Reading
FORWARD

ADVANCED 1

Reading FORWARD

ADVANCED 1

Series Editors Bin-na Yang, Dong-sook Kim

Project Editors Jung-ah Lee, Mina Song, Mi-youn Woo, Jee-young Song, Jeong-eun Han, Eun-young Cho

Contributing Writers Patrick Ferraro, Henry John Amen IV, John Boswell, Jonathan Mcclelland, Paul Nicholas Scherf, Peter Morton

Illustrators Seol-hee Kim, Hyun-jin Choi, Hyo-sil Lee, Seon-me Lee, Dummy

Design Ho-hyun Bang, Hyun-jung Jang, Yeon-joo Kim

Editorial Designer In-sun Lee

Sales Ki-young Han, Kyung-koo Lee, In-gyu Park, Cheol-gyo Jeong. Jin-su Ha, Nam-jun Kim, Woo-hyun Lee

Marketers Hye-sun Park, Kyung-jin Nam, Ji-won Lee, Yeo-jin Kim

Copyright © 2015 by NE Neungyule, Inc.

First Printing 15 June 2015

11th Printing 15 March 2023

ISBN 979-11-253-0800-3

INTRODUCTION

★
★
★

Reading Forward is a six-level series of three progressive steps: Basic, Intermediate, and Advanced. Based on the essential needs of young students, the series focuses on a specific goal: expanding vocabulary and knowledge. This goal guides all of the content and activities in the series. The first step of the series will enlarge vocabulary, and the later steps will increase knowledge. Thus, the series will eventually help students improve their reading comprehension.

Each book of Reading Forward is composed of 20 units. The number of words used in each reading passage is as follows.

Step 3
Reading Forward
Advanced
for Knowledge
1 : 240 – 260 words
2 : 260 – 280 words

Step 2
Reading Forward
Intermediate
for Vocabulary & Knowledge
1 : 200 – 220 words
2 : 220 – 240 words

Step 1
Reading Forward
Basic
for Vocabulary
1 : 150 – 170 words
2 : 170 – 190 words

Key Features of Reading Forward Series

– Current, high-interest topics are developed in an easy way so that students can understand them. These subjects can hold their attention and keep them motivated to read forward.

– Comprehension checkup questions presented in the series are based on standardized test questions. These can help students prepare for English tests at school, as well as official English language tests.

– Each unit is designed to expand knowledge by presenting a further reading passage related to the main topic. Students will build their background knowledge which helps improve their reading comprehension.

FORMAT

Before Reading
The question before each passage allows students to think about the topic by relating it to their lives. It also helps students become interested in the passage before reading it.

Reading
This part serves as the main passage of the unit, and it explains an intriguing and instructive topic in great depth. As students progress through the book, the content of these passages becomes more and more substantial.

Reading Comprehension
The reading is followed by different types of questions, which test understanding of the passage. The various types of questions focus on important reading skills, such as understanding the main idea and organization of the passage, identifying details, and drawing inferences.

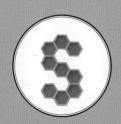

Strategic Summary / Organizer

Each unit includes a strategic summary or organizer of the main reading passage. It gives students a better understanding of the important points and organization of the passage. These exercises focus on further development of effective reading comprehension skills.

Knowledge Expanding

Each unit provides a shorter reading passage related to the topic of the main passage. It elaborates on the content of the main passage by providing additional information or examples, further explanation, or a different point of view on the subject.

Vocabulary Review

A review of the key vocabulary concludes each unit. Three types of exercises test understanding of new words: matching definitions, identifying synonyms and antonyms, and completing sentences with the correct words in context.

TABLE OF CONTENTS

★ ★ ★ ★ ★

Unit 01 JOBS
Reading Art Gallery Curators · 8
Further Reading Art Lending Library · 10

Unit 02 PLANTS
Reading Banyan Tree · 12
Further Reading Redwood · 14

Unit 03 ENVIRONMENT
Reading Biomass Energy · 16
Further Reading Corn Ethanol · 18

Unit 04 ENTERTAINMENT
Reading The Smurfs · 20
Further Reading Smurfs' Language · 22

Unit 05 HISTORY
Reading Carousels · 24
Further Reading Collecting Carousel Horses · 26

Unit 06 SPORTS
Reading An Amazing Race · 28
Further Reading Review · 30

Unit 07 FESTIVALS
Reading Diwali · 32
Further Reading The Kumbh Mela Festival · 34

Unit 08 ORIGINS
Reading The Best Man and Bridesmaids · 36
Further Reading Maids of Honor · 38

Unit 09 LITERATURE
Reading The Wizard of Oz · 40
Further Reading Over the Rainbow · 42

Unit 10 FOOD
Reading Beer · 44
Further Reading The Beer Purity Law · 46

Reading Forward

Unit 11 PEOPLE
Reading   Da Vinci's Kitchen · 48
Further Reading   Da Vinci's Diet · 50

Unit 12 BIOLOGY
Reading   Earworms · 52
Further Reading   Hearing the Ocean in a Seashell · 54

Unit 13 ANIMALS
Reading   Dog Vision · 56
Further Reading   Your Dog and You · 58

Unit 14 HEALTH
Reading   Give Me a Hug! · 60
Further Reading   Free Hugs · 62

Unit 15 FASHION
Reading   Full Figured Fashion Week · 64
Further Reading   Size Zero Debate · 66

Unit 16 PSYCHOLOGY
Reading   The Mother Teresa Effect · 68
Further Reading   The Missionaries of Charity · 70

Unit 17 SPACE
Reading   The Moon · 72
Further Reading   The Moon in Stories · 74

Unit 18 MYSTERIES
Reading   Piri's Map · 76
Further Reading   Admiral Piri · 78

Unit 19 ART
Reading   Claude Monet · 80
Further Reading   Monet and Impressionism · 82

Unit 20 MEDICINE
Reading   New Medicine · 84
Further Reading   Giving Medicine to Dogs · 86

Before Reading
When you visit an art gallery, what helps you understand and enjoy the artwork?

Art Gallery Curators

Bringing art to life — that's my mission as an art gallery curator. Hello! I'm Vivien. Let me tell you about my job.

An art gallery curator does lots of different things. One of my most important tasks is to look after the art collection. I have to know where

5 everything is and check that all of the art is properly cared for. I'm also responsible for organizing exhibitions. ① Four to five times a year, our gallery has special exhibitions. ② When preparing for an exhibition, I choose a theme for it and select what to show. ③ I speak to artists, other museums, and private collectors to borrow their pieces of art for the exhibition.

10 ④ Some artists become famous through special exhibitions of their art. Sometimes I even buy a new piece for the gallery. I have to choose items that people will be interested in seeing now and in the future as well.

The thing I love most about my job, though, is helping people learn about art. I write the labels and brief descriptions that go on the

15 walls next to all the paintings and sculptures. By reading them, people can discover the fascinating stories behind the art. I like to think that I _____ (A) _____.

I love being an art gallery curator. The job is really creative and challenging. It also lets me get close to my favorite thing:

20 art. If you love art and have good communication and organizational skills, an art gallery curator could be the perfect job for you!

1 What is the best title for the passage?

   a. A Variety of Forms of Art
   b. Working to Help People Enjoy Art
   c. Special Exhibitions Held by Art Galleries
   d. Learning about Art History through Books

2 Which sentence is NOT needed in the passage?

   a. ①   *b.* ②   *c.* ③   *d.* ④

3 What can people learn by reading the labels and descriptions next to the artwork?

   _____

4 What is the best choice for blank (A)?

   a. work with world-famous artists
   b. help artists create beautiful artwork
   c. give people chances to make their own artwork
   d. help open people's eyes to the wonderful world of art

5 What is NOT mentioned as a responsibility of an art gallery curator?

   a. Planning art exhibitions
   b. Giving visitors lectures on art
   c. Purchasing artwork for the gallery
   d. Writing short notes about the artwork

6 Write T if the statement is true or F if it's false.

   1) An art gallery curator should make sure the gallery's artwork is in good condition.
   2) To be an art gallery curator, one must be able to create paintings and sculptures.

STRATEGIC ORGANIZER

Fill in the blanks with the correct words.

An Art Gallery Curator

- Takes care of the art _____ of the gallery
- _____ several art exhibitions a year
- _____ new pieces of art for the gallery
- Helps visitors _____ interesting stories about the art
- Requires a love of art, communication and organizational skills

> organizes   collection   find out   buys   researches

★ EXPANDING KNOWLEDGE ★

Did you know that there is a library for art? It is the Art Lending Library, where you can borrow works from an artist's collection for free. There is a wide selection of choices, including ceramics, small sculptures, paintings, drawings, photography, and so on. However, before checking out any artwork, you're required to register at the library. Then, when you choose a piece of art that you want, a librarian brings the piece to your home and installs it in a suitable position. Only the librarian is allowed to touch it. After three months, the librarian comes again to take it back to the library. Through this service, the Art Lending Library helps ordinary people bring _____ (A) _____ into their homes.

1 What is the passage mainly about?

a. Ways of caring for valuable art
b. The rules to follow at a public library
c. A library that lends people works of art
d. The best way to purchase art for your home

2 What is the best choice for blank (A)?

a. their special guests
b. world-famous artists
c. state-of-the-art technology
d. the beauty and enjoyment of art

VOCABULARY REVIEW

A Write the correct word next to its definition.

challenging	label	gallery	task	collection

1 a job or mission someone has to do: _____

2 a group of related things brought together: _____

3 a place where people can see many works of art: _____

4 a list of information attached to what it describes: _____

B Complete each sentence with a word in the box. (Change the form if needed.)

install	lend	creative	register	borrow	exhibition

1 Students have to _____ for classes by the end of this week.

2 The museum is holding a(n) _____ of paintings by Henri Matisse.

3 James is a very _____ person. He always thinks of something new.

4 If you can't buy the book at the bookstore, _____ it from the library.

5 He recently bought a laptop and _____ new antivirus software on it.

C Find the word that has a similar meaning to the underlined word.

1 The actor doesn't like to talk about his <u>private</u> life.

    a. public   *b.* personal   *c.* general   *d.* common

2 The movie is not <u>suitable</u> for children under 12.

    a. funny   *b.* difficult   *c.* exciting   *d.* proper

PLANTS

Before Reading
Is there something special in your country that means a lot to you?

Banyan Tree

A forest is usually made up of many individual trees. But in some cases, a single tree can appear as massive as an entire forest. The Indian banyan

5 tree grows in such a way that it looks like many different trees.

(①) Like most other trees, the banyan begins with a single trunk. (②) These roots create secondary

10 trunks that grow vertically and help support the expanding branches of the tree. (③) This process continues for the life of the tree, so the oldest banyans can cover areas up to 200

15 meters wide. (④)

Thanks to their huge size, banyans have been used as meeting places where people gather to relax in the shade. In fact, the tree's name comes from the word "bania," or merchant, because Indian merchants used to meet under banyans to discuss

20 business. There is even a legend that Alexander the Great's army of 7,000 men once camped under a single banyan tree.

But the banyan's importance in Indian culture goes beyond shelter. It is considered a symbol of eternal life and is often worshipped by Indian people. The banyan is also the national symbol of India. Its connected roots,

25 trunks, and branches represent the unity of the Indian nation. Beyond its symbolic importance, the tree is a source of _____(A)_____ materials as well. Its wood and bark are made into paper, its roots into rope and skin cream, and its seeds are used in medicines. It's easy to see why the banyan tree has been a part of people's lives and stories for such a long time.

1 What is the passage mainly about?

a. How the banyan tree is a natural resource in India

b. How the banyan tree is a plant with an unusual look

c. How the banyan tree is an essential part of the Indian economy

d. How the banyan tree is a meaningful part of Indian life and culture

2 Where would the following sentence best fit?

> Over time, though, the tree sends roots outward along the top of the ground.

a. ①   b. ②   c. ③   d. ④

3 Why does the banyan tree's name originate from "bania," or merchant?

_____

4 What is the best choice for blank (A)?

a. medical

b. practical

c. idealistic

d. mysterious

5 What is NOT mentioned about banyan trees?

a. Their size

b. Their usage

c. Their longevity

d. Their status in India

6 Write T if the statement is true or F if it's false.

1) It is said that Alexander the Great's entire army camped under a banyan tree.

2) The many branches of the banyan tree represent the future generations of India.

STRATEGIC SUMMARY

Fill in the blanks with the correct words.

Banyans are giant trees, _____ as far as 200 meters wide. This makes them a great meeting place for people. In fact, the name banyan comes from the Indian word "bania," or merchant, because Indian merchants held meetings under banyan trees. But banyans are more than just _____ spots. These trees are India's national _____. They are considered sacred. They are also _____; paper, rope, skin cream, and medicines can all be made from banyan trees

> social   useful   symbol   spreading   branches

★ EXPANDING KNOWLEDGE ★

The coast redwood stands high above all other trees in the world. The tallest redwood discovered stands 379.1 feet tall, which is higher than the Big Ben tower in London. Redwoods are also famous for their longevity. Some redwoods live 2,000 years or longer. The trees live so long because their wood has many polyphenols, so bugs and rot don't affect them. Moreover, since their bark has a lot of sticky substances, they are very resistant to fire. Another great feature of redwoods is that they can send water from their leaves down to their roots. They can do this because they absorb fog directly into their leaves. Finally, redwood forests are great for the earth because they remove carbon dioxide from the atmosphere better than any other forest.

1 What is NOT mentioned about redwoods in the passage?

   a. Their usage

   b. Their height

   c. Their water source

   d. Their benefits

2 Write T if the statement is true or F if it's false.

   1) If a fire breaks out, redwoods have a better chance to survive.

   2) Redwood forests help the planet by emitting more carbon dioxide than any other forest.

VOCABULARY REVIEW

A Write the correct word next to its definition.

bark	trunk	eternal	merchant	represent

1 to be a sign or symbol of something: _____

2 the rough material covering the outside of a tree: _____

3 existing or continuing forever or seeming to do so: _____

4 someone who buys and sells products in large amounts: _____

B Complete each sentence with a word in the box. (Change the form if needed.)

entire	absorb	outward	resistant	longevity	substance

1 Please handle this dangerous _____ with great care.

2 Please don't smoke here. The _____ art gallery is non-smoking.

3 Exercising regularly and eating healthy are the secrets to _____.

4 This metal is known to be very _____ to sudden changes in temperature.

5 The construction of houses is spreading _____ from the heart of the town.

C Find the word that has a similar meaning to the underlined word.

1 In the past, some people <u>worshipped</u> animal statues like gods.

    a. hated   *b.* scorned   *c.* thought   *d.* honored

2 They are planning to construct a <u>massive</u> building with 106 floors.

    a. huge   *b.* modern   *c.* artistic   *d.* ordinary

Unit 03 ENVIRONMENT

Before Reading
Have you ever thought of using garbage to make energy?

Biomass Energy

Generally, we consider waste useless and easily throw it away. However, some waste like tree branches, sawdust, and animal waste contains *biomass, which can be reused to produce eco-friendly energy known as biomass energy.

So how can we get energy from material that nobody seems to want? ① One way is to burn the waste in power plants. ② Some people are opposed to building power plants near houses due to safety concerns. ③ The heat from burning the waste is used to boil water, which creates steam. ④ Then the energy of the steam operates generators to make electricity. Another way is to use the methane gas that is created by the
15 decomposing garbage in landfills or the waste of cattle, pigs, and chickens. This gas is collected and then burned to produce energy.

Producing and consuming biomass energy is helpful in several ways. First, we can reduce the amount of garbage by burning some of it. If we
20 don't, the garbage will end up in landfills and possibly cause contamination. _____(A)_____, using biomass can reduce the use of fossil fuels such as oil, coal, and natural gas. Biomass is even environmentally friendly because it releases less carbon dioxide than fossil fuels. Furthermore, it cuts methane gas, one of the main causes of the greenhouse effect.

25 These days, it is getting harder and more expensive to obtain energy resources. So why don't we use biomass instead? It is economical, and it will never dry up as long as plants and animals live on Earth.

*biomass: biological material made from plants and animals

16

1 What is the best title for the passage?

 a. Stop Using Fossil Fuels and Save Earth!

 b. Save Your Energy and Save Your Money

 c. A Way of Getting Great Value from Waste

 d. Biomass: One of Many Causes of Global Warming

2 Which sentence is NOT needed in the passage?

 a. ①   *b.* ②   *c.* ③   *d.* ④

3 What is the best choice for blank (A)?

 a. However   *b.* Therefore

 c. In addition   *d.* For example

4 Why is using biomass instead of fossil fuels eco-friendly?

_____

5 What does the underlined part mean?

 a. Plants and animals make the soil wet.

 b. Plants and animals will survive on Earth forever.

 c. Plants and animals can't live without a water supply.

 d. Plants and animals will keep providing us with biomass.

6 What is NOT mentioned as a benefit of biomass energy?

 a. A decrease in garbage

 b. Less use of fossil fuels

 c. No production of methane gas

 d. Availability of a cheap energy resource

Fill in the blanks with the correct words.

Biomass energy is fuel we can get from waste. It is produced by _____ waste in power plants. It can also be made by using methane gas from landfill sites and animal waste. It has several advantages. First, it reduces _____ that would be buried in landfills. Second, it cuts the use of _____ and reduces the amount of greenhouse gas emissions. Last, it is a(n) _____ energy resource. Therefore, it is much more efficient than using fossil fuels.

> cheap   garbage   burning   electricity   fossil fuels

★ EXPANDING KNOWLEDGE ★

Did you know we can get a type of fuel from corn? It's corn *ethanol, which can be produced by changing the sugars in corn into alcohol. Corn ethanol is a good fuel for use in some kinds of engines. It's also used to run vehicles and is of great use in the chemical industry. Furthermore, corn ethanol is believed to be eco-friendly, because it releases lower amounts of greenhouse gases than fossil fuels. However, it's not an efficient fuel. To produce 25 gallons of ethanol, 450 pounds of corn is needed. That's as much as a person could eat in a year! So as we use more corn ethanol, we need much more corn. As a result, the price of corn rises, which affects everything that is produced using corn.

*ethanol: a type of alcohol in drinks, also used as a fuel

1 **What is the passage mainly about?**

a. The popularity of corn as food

b. The need for a new kind of fuel

c. The pros and cons of corn ethanol

d. How to prevent the greenhouse effect

2 **Write T if the statement is true or F if it's false.**

1) Corn ethanol is criticized because it creates more greenhouse gases than fossil fuels do.

2) The more we use corn ethanol, the more expensive corn becomes.

VOCABULARY REVIEW

A Write the correct word next to its definition.

operate	useless	release	decompose	landfill

1 to let something out: _____

2 to control a machine or help it to work: _____

3 to be destroyed or decay through natural processes: _____

4 an area of land where waste is buried under the ground: _____

B Complete each sentence with a word in the box. (Change the form if needed.)

industry	steam	opposed	reuse	efficient	electricity

1 When water is heated to over 100°C, it turns to _____.

2 You can help protect the environment by _____ plastic bags.

3 The tourism _____ of the country was in decline due to the earthquake.

4 Abraham Lincoln was the president who was _____ to slavery in the U.S.

5 Closing doors tightly is a(n) _____ way of keeping the heat from escaping.

C Find the word that has a similar meaning to the underlined word.

1 We need to <u>reduce</u> the cost of production this year.

    a. allow   *b.* lower   *c.* increase   *d.* encourage

2 I tried hard to <u>obtain</u> a chance to study at Harvard University.

    a. get   *b.* lose   *c.* store   *d.* research

ENTERTAINMENT

Before Reading

Who is your favorite character from a movie, novel, or cartoon?

The Smurfs

Do you know *Les Schtroumpfs*? They are small and blue, they wear white caps, and they live in mushroom-shaped houses hidden deep in the forest. These popular cartoon characters were created by the Belgian cartoonist Peyo in 1958. They are known as the Smurfs in English.

5   Originally, they were secondary characters in another comic strip, *The Flute with Six Holes*. After the story was published, the Smurfs became so popular that they were given their own comic strip. Concerning their name, there is another interesting fact. One day, Peyo suddenly forgot the word for "salt" while eating with a friend. He asked for the *schtroumpf* instead,
10   and this made-up word soon became a joke between him and his friend. Eventually, the *Schtroumpfs* became the name of the characters.

Over time, the Smurfs grew popular around the world. In 2008, their 50th anniversary was celebrated. In their honor, Belgium created a special five-euro coin with their image on it. UNICEF also marked the anniversary
15   by sending the Smurfs on a one-year worldwide tour to raise money. Plain Smurf figures were painted by famous people and then auctioned off, earning more than 100,000 euros for UNICEF's educational programs.

Despite their old age, the Smurfs continue to be successful year after year. Pop songs,
20   videos, and computer games featuring them sell well all around the world. There are Smurf television shows, Smurf movies, Smurf theme parks, and even plays featuring the Smurfs! It seems as though people will never _____(A)_____ Peyo's charming, blue cartoon characters.

1 **What is the best title for the passage?**

 a. How Peyo Created the Smurfs

 b. The Smurfs: A Symbol of Belgium

 c. The Birth and Popularity of the Smurfs

 d. The Relationship between UNICEF and the Smurfs

2 **How did the Smurfs get their name?**

 a. Peyo ran an idea contest for comic strip readers.

 b. Peyo named them after the French word for salt.

 c. Peyo and his friend held several meetings to name them.

 d. Peyo accidentally invented a new word for salt and liked it.

3 **How did UNICEF celebrate the 50th anniversary of the Smurfs?**

_____

4 **What is the best choice for blank (A)?**

 a. be ignored by   *b.* grow tired of

 c. be inspired by   *d.* get accustomed to

5 **What is NOT true according to the passage?**

 a. The Smurfs were not main characters at first.

 b. Various kinds of coins were made to celebrate the Smurfs' anniversary.

 c. The Smurfs' 50th anniversary benefited UNICEF's educational programs.

 d. The Smurfs can be seen in various media forms.

6 **What can be inferred from the passage?**

 a. The Smurfs were fairies in a Belgian folktale.

 b. Celebrities got paid for painting Smurf figures.

 c. *The Flute with Six Holes* became popular as well.

 d. Belgians have respect and affection for the Smurfs.

Fill in the blanks with the correct words.

The Smurfs

The origin
- Were created as secondary characters and became _____
- Were given a _____ of their own
- Got their name from a _____ Peyo made asking for salt

For the 50th anniversary celebration
- Appeared on a special five-euro coin in 2008
- Had a worldwide UNICEF _____ for a year

Continued popularity
- Have been _____ in songs, games, TV shows, movies, etc.

> tour   strip   publish   featured   mistake   popular

★ EXPANDING KNOWLEDGE ★

The Belgian animated series *The Smurfs* has been an international hit for over five decades. But did you know that, originally, the Smurfs had their very own language? One of the major characteristics of their language was that the term "smurf" often replaced other words. For example, when one character tried to say, "I'm going to the woods today," the expression became "I'm smurfing to the smurf today." What the word "smurf" meant had to be worked out from the context and intonation. But this sometimes caused great confusion to people who watched the show. So the language had to be simplified to make it less confusing. However, the word "smurf" is still frequently used in the series today.

SMURF!

1 What is the passage mainly about?

a. The confusing but interesting language of the Smurfs
b. The basic rules that are found in the Smurfs' language
c. What made the Smurfs' language popular with children
d. The importance of context and intonation in the Smurfs' language

2 Write T if the statement is true or F if it's false.

1) The term "smurf" can be used instead of other words in the Smurfs' language.
2) The word "smurf" was used less often in earlier versions of *The Smurfs* than it is now.

VOCABULARY REVIEW

A Write the correct word next to its definition.

| decade | replace | feature | anniversary | secondary |

1 a period of ten years: _____

2 to substitute one thing for another: _____

3 included with but less important than something else: _____

4 to show something as an important part of something: _____

B Complete each sentence with a word in the box. (Change the form if needed.)

| strip | simplify | publish | originally | confusing | characteristic |

1 This magazine has been _____ twice a month since 2010.

2 A common _____ of traditional *hanbok* is the use of beautiful colors.

3 The road signs were _____, so we had to ask someone for directions.

4 This system can _____ the process of completing the complicated task.

5 I _____ planned to travel for a year, but later I found I couldn't afford it.

C Find the word that has a similar meaning to the underlined word.

1 He <u>eventually</u> got a job as an actor and became very successful.

    a. hardly   *b.* finally   *c.* rapidly   *d.* fortunately

2 If you want to lose weight, you may need to exercise more <u>frequently</u>.

    a. often   *b.* seldom   *c.* exactly   *d.* quickly

Carousels

People are standing in front of the merry-go-round in the amusement park. The flashing lights, bright colors, and loud circus music all catch their attention. They feel like getting on one of the painted horses
5 and going around and around. It is hard to believe that such an innocent children's ride started off as _____(A)_____.

In the 12th century, Turkish soldiers played a game on horseback to prepare for battle. The Spanish
10 warriors who saw the game named it *carosella*, which means "a little war." They brought the game to Europe, and it eventually became a popular way to show one's horse riding skills. Many years later, a Frenchman built a machine based on this game. It had carved wooden horses held up by chains coming out of a
15 central pole. The carousels today come from his invention.

Over time, carousels evolved from simple rides to huge machines. However, it was not until Americans began making carousels in the 1860s that they became works of art. _____(B)_____ European carousels, American carousels were beautiful, with detailed, hand-carved horses, lions,
20 and even dragons. This was the golden age of carousels. Soon, the carousel was the main focus of amusement parks around the country.

_____(C)_____, by the time of the Great Depression in the 1930s, carousels had fallen out of favor, and many were damaged or destroyed. But as the economy got better, so did the technology for making carousels. Instead of using hand-carved wooden horses, makers of carousels started to use fiberglass and aluminum. Today, carousels are once again an essential children's ride.

1 What is the best title for the passage?

   a. The Varieties of Children's Carousels

   b. The Materials Used to Make Carousels

   c. The Characteristics of Modern Carousels

   d. The History and Evolution of the Carousel

2 What is the best choice for blank (A)?

   a. a weapon for war

   b. a training tool for war

   c. an invention for horses

   d. a game for noblemen's leisure

3 How was the *carosella* game used after Spanish warriors brought it to Europe?

_____

4 What is the best pair for blanks (B) and (C)?

	(B)	(C)
a.	Unlike	— However
b.	In spite of	— Moreover
c.	Similar to	— Though
d.	In addition to	— Otherwise

5 What is true about carousels early in the 20th century?

   a. Their earlier popularity declined.

   b. They were made by female artists.

   c. They were well preserved in museums.

   d. They became a foundation of economic recovery.

6 Write T if the statement is true or F if it's false.

   1) Turkish soldiers carved horses as a game before going to war.

   2) Modern carousels came from a French machine with wooden horses, chains, and poles.

Fill in the blanks with the correct words.

Carousels

In the Middle Ages
- In Turkey: A game played on horses to _____ soldiers
- In Spain: Named the game and used it to show _____
- In France: Made a(n) _____ based on the game

In the 19th century: The golden age of carousels
- Featuring hand-carved wooden animals with beautiful _____

In the 20th century
- Once _____ but later became popular again

details   horsemanship   machine   unwanted   train   evolved

★ EXPANDING KNOWLEDGE ★

 Did you know you can own your own carousel horses? Actually, they are popular items to collect. Carousel horses are regarded as unique works of art created by skilled artists. Most horses generally come painted, but some people prefer to paint their horses themselves to give them their own personal touch. Carousel horses can be purchased from a variety of places. While most people look online these days, there are also great treasures to be found at antique stores and local auctions. The horses are often given as a child's birthday present, although many purchase them simply to give their homes an antique look. In some cases, carousel horses are passed down from generation to generation, staying in a family for many years.

1 **What is the best title for the passage?**

   a. Reasons to Buy Carousel Horses
   b. Antique Furniture for Your House
   c. Artists Who Make Carousel Horses
   d. Carousel Horses as Valuable Collectables

2 **What is NOT mentioned as a place to buy carousel horses?**

   a. Online
   b. Theme parks
   c. Antique stores
   d. Auctions

VOCABULARY REVIEW

A Choose the correct word for each definition.

carve	warrior	invention	generation	antique

1 someone who fights in a war or battle: _____

2 a group of people born around the same time: _____

3 to make an object by cutting it from solid wood or stone: _____

4 an old object that is valuable because it is rare or beautiful: _____

B Complete each sentence with a word in the box. (Change the form if needed.)

pass down	innocent	destroy	go around	evolve	purchase

1 The building has been completely _____ by the fire.

2 The computer has _____ from a simple calculating machine.

3 He likes to take pictures of the _____ smiles of little children.

4 The students learned in science class that the earth _____ the sun.

5 My grandparents did their best to _____ good values to their children.

C Find the word that has a similar meaning to the underlined word.

1 The showcase was filled with a variety of products.

    a. unique   *b.* various   *c.* expensive   *d.* interesting

2 Jenny's ambition is to own her own business.

    a. sell   *b.* earn   *c.* have   *d.* collect

An Amazing Race

If you are looking for an extreme adventure or a serious challenge, the 4 Deserts Race is the obvious choice. It is a world-class sporting event open to everyone.

5　　The 4 Deserts Race is a series of seven-day, 250-kilometer races across the driest, hottest, coldest, and windiest places on the earth. (①) The four deserts are the Gobi Desert in China, the Atacama Desert in Chile, the Sahara Desert in Egypt, and lastly, Antarctica. (②) The total distance of the race is 1,000 kilometers. (③) But they also experience unique climates, enjoy beautiful scenery, and encounter ancient cultures. (④)

10　　The runners are given water to drink and places to sleep, and they are monitored by teams of medical professionals. However, they must carry all their own food and equipment as they run through some of the harshest weather conditions on the planet. At the end of the race, more than 50 hours may separate the fastest runners from the slowest ones. However, for
15　most of the competitors, this race is about much more than winning and losing.

By the time the 4 Deserts Race is over, the runners, who come from a wide range of cultures and speak many different languages, will have shared an amazing experience. Because of this, they will leave feeling as though
20　they are part of a new, special family. In the words of Mary Gadams, who organized the 4 Deserts Race in 2002, "These events were always meant to be one of the most remarkable journeys on the earth. I believe that anyone who takes on the challenge will never be the same."

1 What is the best title for the passage?

   a. Tips on Winning a Challenging Race

   b. What Makes Long-Distance Races Difficult

   c. The 4 Deserts Race: A Challenging Journey

   d. Why People Participate in the 4 Deserts Race

2 Where would the following sentence best fit?

> As they run, race participants test their limits both mentally and physically.

   a. ①   *b.* ②   *c.* ③   *d.* ④

3 What does the underlined part mean?

   a. Surviving the race is the ultimate goal.

   b. Winning the race is not that important.

   c. Finishing the race is a matter of chance.

   d. To win or lose is completely up to the runners.

4 How do the participants feel after the race with people from different backgrounds?

_____

5 What is NOT true about the 4 Deserts Race?

   a. People from various countries take part in it.

   b. Participants can have unique experiences during the race.

   c. Participants cannot get any medical aid during the race.

   d. Participants must carry their own food and equipment.

6 What is NOT mentioned about the 4 Deserts Race?

   a. The length of each race

   b. Where the races take place

   c. Who created the race

   d. The number of participants

Fill in the blanks with the correct words.

The 4 Deserts Race consists of four separate week-long 250-kilometer races in the toughest places on the earth. During the course of the event, participants push themselves to their _____ while experiencing the world's _____ places. During the event, runners are given only water and places to sleep, and they must carry the rest of their _____. For many people, the race is not about winning or losing. Rather, the shared _____ of the race is what counts. After completing the 4 Deserts Race, a person will never be the same.

| limits | country | harshest | equipment | experience |

★ EXPANDING KNOWLEDGE ★

I took the longest walk of my life yesterday. My 17 hours of continuous walking was stopped only by brief breaks for food. I began my march at 8:00 a.m. with a horrible trek across 7 kilometers of salt plains. Afterward, the terrain was much more comfortable, allowing me to walk while taking pictures of the stunning scenery. By mid-afternoon, the sun had turned into a scorching ball of fire. Luckily, a few clouds provided some relief from the heat. By late afternoon, the sun started to set. I changed into my warmer clothes and kept walking for hours in the dark without seeing any other life. I had the whole desert to myself! As I walked, I thought about my life and future. This is exactly why I signed up for this race — to learn about myself.

1 **What is the purpose of the passage?**

a. To criticize a challenging sport
b. To share a personal experience
c. To give some tips for desert trips
d. To persuade others to join a race

2 **Write T if the statement is true or F if it's false.**

1) The writer walked without resting except for quick meals.
2) The writer scarcely had time for self-reflection after sunset.

VOCABULARY REVIEW

A Write the correct word next to its definition.

| extreme | monitor | obvious | encounter | challenge |

1 very great in degree: _____

2 clear to almost anyone: _____

3 to meet or experience something: _____

4 to watch and check a situation to see how it changes: _____

B Complete each sentence with a word in the box. (Change the form if needed.)

| relief | scenery | organize | separate | continuous | participant |

1 The number of _____ in the marathon was over 10,000.

2 At that time, the channel _____ the island from the mainland.

3 The politician is planning to _____ a new political party next fall.

4 I was able to succeed as an artist due to my mother's _____ support.

5 How about stopping the car to enjoy the beautiful _____ for a while?

C Find the word that has a similar meaning to the underlined word.

1 My car is not suitable for driving over rocky terrain.

    a. roads   *b.* land   *c.* coasts   *d.* mountains

2 The actress looked stunning in that black dress.

    a. happy   *b.* lonely   *c.* nervous   *d.* beautiful

Before Reading
How do people all over the world celebrate the fall harvest?

Diwali

In October or November of each year, villages across India are lit by the soft light of clay lamps. This is a sure sign that Diwali has come again.

Diwali is the most significant holiday in the country, similar to Christmas in the Christian world. The name comes from a combination of
5 two words: *deepa*, meaning "clay lamp," and *avali*, meaning "row." As you may assume, lights play a major role in this holiday.

Diwali was originally celebrated by Hindus to mark the year's final harvest. Hindus from different regions use different stories to explain the meaning of Diwali. But one theme is always present: the defeat of evil by
10 good and the start of a prosperous new year!

Today, Indians of all faiths take part in Diwali events. In general, these include putting up decorations made of electric lights, candles, and flowers, and then seeing family and feasting with them. More specifically, each of the five days of Diwali is meant to be celebrated in a _____(A)_____ way.
15 On the first day, people clean their houses and shop for holiday supplies. The second day is the time to decorate the home. The third day is the main holiday, when families gather to pray, eat, and watch fireworks. On the fourth day, they exchange gifts. Then the fifth day is traditionally the time for brothers and sisters to visit one another's homes.

Diwali is one of the most exciting times of year to visit India. The countless decorations turn entire cities into explosions of light and color. Wouldn't you like to take part in this "festival of lights"?

1 What is the best title for the passage?

    a. Diwali: India's Festival of Lights

    b. The History and Origin of Diwali

    c. Christmas and Diwali, Festival Rivals

    d. The Relationship between Festivals and Religions

2 What is the main theme of Diwali?

    _____

3 What is the best choice for blank (A)?

    a. plain   *b.* similar

    c. serious   *d.* different

4 What is NOT a way to celebrate Diwali?

    a. Visiting the home of one's best friend

    b. Baking bread and eating it with one's family

    c. Knitting a scarf and giving it to one's mother

    d. Buying ornaments and making one's house beautiful

5 What is NOT mentioned about Diwali?

    a. When it is celebrated

    b. What its name means

    c. How it is celebrated

    d. Which other countries celebrate it

6 Write T if the statement is true or F if it's false.

    1) Stories about Diwali's origins differ among regions.

    2) Decorations used for Diwali need to be made of natural materials.

Fill in the blanks with the correct words.

Diwali — The _____ of good over evil and a new year's prosperous beginning

Details • _____ in October or November
• Means "clay lamps in a row"
• Originally celebrated the year's final _____

For celebration • Clean and _____ homes
• Eat, pray, and watch fireworks
• Exchange _____ and visit the homes of siblings

gifts	happens	harvest	faith	triumph	decorate

★ EXPANDING KNOWLEDGE ★

For more than 40 days, people celebrate the Kumbh Mela, one of the most important festivals in Hinduism. During the festival, they dance, sing, and do charity work. However, the major event is bathing in four sacred rivers in India on specific dates. Hindus believe that bathing in the rivers allows their sins of this life to be forgiven. This festival attracts people to India from all over the world. It takes place every three years, and the four rivers take turns holding it. Therefore, the festival is held at each river once every twelve years; this is called the Purna Kumbh Mela. After twelve Purna Kumbh Mela, the Maha Kumbh Mela is held. The last one was held in 2001 with 100 million participants.

1 What is the best title for the passage?

a. What Is the Kumbh Mela?

b. How Many Festivals Are There in India?

c. What Is the Biggest Festival in the World?

d. Why Do Hindus Celebrate the Kumbh Mela?

2 Write T if the statement is true or F if it's false.

1) The Kumbh Mela is held at four sacred rivers at the same time.

2) The Maha Kumbh Mela is celebrated every 144 years.

VOCABULARY REVIEW

A Write the correct word next to its definition.

forgive	decorate	assume	feast	prosperous

1 rich and successful: _____

2 to eat and drink a lot and enjoy it very much: _____

3 to make an object more attractive by putting something nice on it: _____

4 to stop feeling angry with someone for something they have done: _____

B Complete each sentence with a word in the box. (Change the form if needed.)

exchange	combination	harvest	region	take part in	bathe

1 It is _____ season, so the markets are full of fresh fruit.

2 When you _____, use the body wash for your skin type.

3 More than 5,000 people will _____ the race on Thursday.

4 A(n) _____ of exercise and dieting will help you lose weight.

5 The meeting was held to _____ information with other teams.

C Find the word that has a similar meaning to the underlined word.

1 In India, all temples are considered <u>sacred</u> places.

    a. scary   *b.* boring   *c.* holy   *d.* safe

2 The researchers made a <u>significant</u> discovery to prevent the disease.

    a. another   *b.* important   *c.* normal   *d.* individual

Before Reading
Have you seen a group of people in similar clothes at some weddings?

The Best Man and Bridesmaids

Who are the stars of a wedding? It's the bride and groom, of course. But modern wedding parties include other important people. On the groom's

5   side, there is the best man, and on the bride's side, there are the bridesmaids. These people support the bride and groom during the wedding and help arrange the ceremony. But their original

10 roles were much more difficult.

The tradition of the best man dates back to early Germanic times. During this era, marriage was not always romantic. <u>A man would often capture a woman from a neighboring village and force her into marriage!</u>

15 This was hard to do, so the groom-to-be needed someone to assist him. Thus, he chose the "best man" he knew to help him get married. It was also the job of the best man to protect the groom during and after the wedding. If the bride's family came to rescue her, there was sure to be a fight.

Bridesmaids have existed almost as long as the best man. In ancient

20 Rome, a law said ten people had to witness a wedding. Otherwise, it wasn't legal. So the bride's friends and family attended the wedding as witnesses. Later, bridesmaids started performing a different function. People thought that evil spirits came to weddings to cause bad luck for the bride and groom. Bridesmaids were supposed to trick the spirits by wearing dresses identical to the bride's so that the spirits wouldn't know who was getting married. Today, bridesmaids still dress similarly to the bride, fooling the spirits!

1 What is the best title for the passage?

    a. Who the Best Man and Bridesmaids Are

    b. The History of the Best Man and Bridesmaids

    c. How to Choose the Best Man and Bridesmaids

    d. Difficult Roles of the Best Man and Bridesmaids

2 What can be inferred from the underlined sentence?

    a. The Germanic people were naturally aggressive and hostile.

    b. Germanic women had to hire a bodyguard to protect themselves.

    c. Wars often broke out between neighboring villages in Germany in the past.

    d. Many marriages took place without mutual agreement in early Germanic times.

3 Besides helping the groom capture a woman, what did the best man do for the groom?

_____

4 What is NOT mentioned as a role of bridesmaids?

    a. To help arrange the wedding ceremony

    b. To protect the bride and groom physically

    c. To attend the wedding as a witness

    d. To fool evil spirits by wearing the same dress as the bride

5 What is NOT true according to the passage?

    a. The best man stands by the groom during the wedding ceremony.

    b. The roles of bridesmaids and the best man have changed.

    c. The way people find marriage partners has changed a lot over the years.

    d. It's no longer necessary for the best man and bridesmaids to attend the wedding ceremony.

6 Write T if the statement is true or F if it's false.

    1) In early Germanic times, the groom selected a man whom he knew to help him.

    2) The use of the best man and bridesmaids is based on old wedding traditions.

Fill in the blanks with the correct words.

The Best Man and Bridesmaids

Their roles today
• Helping the bride and groom _____ the wedding ceremony

Their roles in the past
1 The best man
  • Helping the groom _____ his bride from another village
  • Keeping the groom _____ from the bride's family
2 Bridesmaids
  • Being legal _____ for the wedding
  • Dressing _____ to the bride to trick evil spirits

| safe | rescue | witnesses | arrange | capture | identically |

★ EXPANDING KNOWLEDGE ★

When a woman gets married in North America, she often chooses several bridesmaids. And only one of these women will be the maid of honor, who is usually the bride's best friend or sister. She generally has several responsibilities. _____(A)_____ attending the wedding, she often helps the bride with everything from sending invitations to choosing a dress. On the day of the wedding, the maid of honor provides the bride with practical and emotional support. She may keep the groom's wedding ring during the ceremony. Also, she may be asked to be a legal witness of the ceremony. At the reception, the maid of honor usually offers a toast to the newlyweds.

1 What is the best choice for blank (A)?

a. Instead of
b. In spite of
c. Regardless of
d. In addition to

2 What is NOT mentioned as a duty of a maid of honor?

a. To participate in the wedding ceremony
b. To accompany the bride as she shops for her wedding dress
c. To keep the wedding ring until it is needed during the ceremony
d. To arrange the reception after the wedding ceremony

VOCABULARY REVIEW

A Write the correct word next to its definition.

neighboring	legal	rescue	arrange	witness

1 allowed by law: _____

2 near or next to something: _____

3 to make plans or prepare for something: _____

4 to save someone from a dangerous or harmful situation: _____

B Complete each sentence with a word in the box. (Change the form if needed.)

bride	fight	ancient	capture	identical	function

1 The beautiful _____ tried not to cry during the wedding ceremony.

2 In the _____ tomb, they found lots of gold coins and valuable jewels.

3 Navy forces try to _____ pirates who are threatening the security of the sea.

4 The _____ between the players became so fierce that no one dared to stop it.

5 The houses on the street looked _____, so I didn't know which house was Mary's.

C Find the word that has a similar meaning to the underlined word.

1 The new employee <u>assisted</u> me in completing this project.

a. helped   b. upgraded   c. answered   d. followed

2 Charles Dickens was one of the most famous writers of the Victorian <u>era</u>.

a. war   b. region   c. nation   d. period

Before Reading

What if you were suddenly separated from your family in an accident?

The Wizard of Oz

Dorothy was playing with her dog, Toto, while Aunt Em washed the dishes. Suddenly, Uncle Henry hurried into the kitchen with an alarmed look on his face.

"There's a tornado coming," he yelled. "Go down into the cellar!" Aunt Em pulled open the cellar door and ran down the stairs. Dorothy started to follow, but just then Toto jumped from her arms and ran away. By the time Dorothy was able to catch him, something strange was happening.

First, the house began to shake, and then it began to spin. And finally, it began to slowly rise up into the air. They were in the middle of the tornado! The house rose up to the top of the tornado and remained there, rocking like a ship on a stormy sea. Toto was barking in fear, but Dorothy held him tightly in her arms and waited to see what would happen next.

They must have traveled for miles and miles. The wind was blowing so loudly that Dorothy couldn't hear a thing. It seemed as if the house would never come back down. And when it did, what would happen? Would it be smashed to pieces? Dorothy didn't know. Then hours passed and nothing happened. Slowly, her fear began to go away. Dorothy stopped worrying and resolved to wait calmly and see what would happen.

Finally, she walked to her bedroom and climbed into her bed.

_____(A)_____ the house was swaying and the wind was howling, the moment Dorothy closed her eyes she fell fast asleep.

1 What is the best title for the passage?

   a. Dorothy Saves Her Dog

   b. Dorothy Overcomes Her Difficulties

   c. Dorothy Is Swept Away by a Tornado

   d. Dorothy Moves Away from Her Family

2 What did Dorothy's aunt do when she noticed the tornado was coming?

_____

3 What is the best choice for blank (A)?

   a. Unless   *b.* Because

   c. As long as   *d.* Even though

4 How did Dorothy's feelings change throughout the story?

   a. excited → anxious

   b. sorrowful → bored

   c. frightened → calm

   d. astonished → delightful

5 What can NOT be inferred from the passage?

   a. Dorothy is staying with her uncle and aunt.

   b. Aunt Em doesn't like Dorothy or Toto.

   c. Dorothy couldn't go to the cellar because of Toto.

   d. The house ended up far away from where it was originally.

6 Write T if the statement is true or F if it's false.

   1) The person who first knew about the tornado was Dorothy's aunt.

   2) Dorothy's house was lifted up and destroyed by the tornado.

Fill in the blanks with the correct words.

One day, when Dorothy was with her Aunt Em, Uncle Henry, and dog Toto, a dangerous _____ came toward the house. Aunt Em and Uncle Henry ran into the _____ for safety. However, Toto went into the house and Dorothy followed him. Then the house got picked up by the tornado! The tornado lasted for hours and _____ the house far away. At first, Dorothy was _____, but later she stopped worrying. She climbed into her bed and even fell _____.

> scared   asleep   barked   cellar   tornado   blew

★ EXPANDING KNOWLEDGE ★

You are probably familiar with the song that begins, "Somewhere over the rainbow, way up high ..." Did you know that this song, titled "Over the Rainbow," is from the 1939 movie *The Wizard of Oz*? The main character, Dorothy, is a curious girl from a small town who dreams of visiting a different, exciting world. In the movie, she sings this song while dreaming of a beautiful place located over the rainbow. Judy Garland, the actress and singer who played Dorothy, sang the song herself in the movie. The song "Over the Rainbow" gained great popularity, and it won the Academy Award for Best Original Song that year. Since then, this song has been sung by countless musicians and has become a classic.

1 **What is the best title for the passage?**

    a. The Success of *The Wizard of Oz*
    b. Why "Over the Rainbow" Became a Classic
    c. The History of the Song "Over the Rainbow"
    d. The Hidden Meaning of the Song "Over the Rainbow"

2 **Write T if the statement is true or F if it's false.**

    1) The song "Over the Rainbow" from the 1939 film *The Wizard of Oz* was a great hit.
    2) Judy Garland, who played Dorothy in the film, won an Academy Award for Best Song.

VOCABULARY REVIEW

A Write the correct word next to its definition.

cellar	spin	classic	sway	howl

1 to swing or move slowly from side to side: _____

2 an underground room used for storing things: _____

3 to make a long loud sound like a wolf or dog: _____

4 something that has been popular for a long time: _____

B Complete each sentence with a word in the box. (Change the form if needed.)

stormy	tightly	yell	curious	smash	bark

1 It is natural for children to be _____ about their environment.

2 The dogs are very aggressive, and they always _____ at strangers.

3 I _____ for help to someone across the street because I was in danger.

4 No one knew who _____ the dishes on the table into pieces last night.

5 Nancy was so happy to see him that she hugged him _____ in her arms.

C Find the word that has a similar meaning to the underlined word.

1 Ted resolved not to give up looking for a good job.

    a. hoped   *b.* decided   *c.* denied   *d.* planned

2 We had the chance to see countless types of fish under the sea.

    a. several   *b.* common   *c.* colorful   *d.* numerous

Beer

Imagine a yellowish liquid with bubbles. This is not soda as you may have been thinking. It is an alcoholic beverage with an 8,000-year history — beer.

Around 6000 B.C., the Sumerians ate bread made of barley or wheat. One day, some bread got wet, perhaps from spilled water or rain. This wet
5 bread was affected by natural yeast in the air. Soon, the bread was covered in foam and became so soaked that it could be drunk rather than chewed. People who drank it liked the sweet and pleasant flavor and started to make "liquid bread" for consumption. This was _____(A)_____.

It is said that 17 to 20 different kinds of beer were made in ancient
10 Sumer and Egypt. Women drank beer made from wheat with honey or cinnamon added, and men enjoyed bitter beer made from barley. ① Ancient governments managed beer making, and each day they gave all citizens a certain amount. ② Also, beer mixed with medicine, herbs, or spices was used to treat stomach problems. ③ As food couldn't be refrigerated, it often
15 went bad, which led to stomachaches and nausea. ④ People in the beer-making industry were highly respected, and they, like priests, didn't have to serve in the military during war.

Since that time, beer making has been popular in many societies. It spread across Europe during the Middle Ages, though only the rich could
20 enjoy it. These days, however, beer has once again become the drink for people of all classes. Specific regions and countries make beer with different ingredients and methods, and currently there are countless varieties available.

1 What is the best title for the passage?

  a. The Various Purposes of Beer
  b. The Origin and History of Beer
  c. The Varieties and Features of Beer
  d. The Favorite Drink of Ancient People

2 What is the best choice for blank (A)?

  a. the first liquor
  b. the birth of beer
  c. the problem of yeast
  d. the ingredients of beer

3 Which sentence is NOT needed in the passage?

  a. ①   b. ②   c. ③   d. ④

4 Why are there lots of kinds of beer nowadays?

_____

5 What is NOT mentioned in the passage?

  a. How the first beer tasted
  b. When beer was first made
  c. Who drank beer
  d. How much beer has been consumed

6 Write T if the statement is true or F if it's false.

  1) Ancient men and women drank the same kind of beer.
  2) Only a few people could enjoy beer in the Middle Ages.

Fill in the blanks with the correct words.

The history of beer stretches back 8,000 years. Around 6000 B.C., some bread accidentally got wet. Yeast in the air caused the bread to become foamy and _____. Thus beer was born. Women preferred sweet wheat beer, while men preferred _____ barley beer. Ancient governments considered beer making very _____. In fact, beer makers didn't have to _____ in the military. Since then, a lot more societies have made beer. People throughout the world today _____ drinking beer.

```
enjoy    bitter    serve    respect    drinkable    important
```

★ EXPANDING KNOWLEDGE ★

In 1516, two Bavarian noblemen in what is now Germany made a law stating that beer could only be made from barley, water, and hops. This eventually became known as the Beer Purity Law. However, keeping beer pure was not its original intent. It was actually written to stop beer makers from using more valuable grains, such as wheat and rye. By restricting grains to barley to make beer, the law ensured such valuable grains were reserved for use by bakers. However, after World War II, the law became a marketing tool to promote the quality of German beers. Thanks to this law, German beer is now known worldwide for its superior quality and consistency of flavor.

1 What is NOT mentioned in the passage?

a. The creators of the Beer Purity Law
b. The original purpose of the Beer Purity Law
c. The influence of the Beer Purity Law on German beer
d. The success of beer made by Bavarian beer makers

2 Write T if the statement is true or F if it's false.

1) Before the Beer Purity Law, beer makers used to make beer with wheat and rye.
2) The Beer Purity Law was used to promote good-quality German beers.

VOCABULARY REVIEW

A Write the correct word next to its definition.

chew	liquid	specific	nobleman	consistency

1 the quality of things being the same: _____

2 a person from a family of high social rank: _____

3 a substance that is not a solid or a gas, such as water: _____

4 to bite food into smaller pieces with your teeth before swallowing it: _____

B Complete each sentence with a word in the box. (Change the form if needed.)

nausea	citizen	ingredient	beverage	valuable	consumption

1 More than half of the _____ voted against the new tax law.

2 As the price of milk increased, the _____ of it declined sharply.

3 Potatoes, eggs, and milk are the main _____ of this delicious dish.

4 Free _____, including juice and coffee, were provided to all guests.

5 While riding the bus on the bumpy road, Sandra got sick with _____.

C Find the word that has a similar meaning to the underlined word.

1 The lead singer in the band is <u>currently</u> popular with young women.

    a. now   *b.* very   *c.* once   *d.* suddenly

2 Cheese made in Switzerland is <u>superior</u> in quality.

    a. equal   *b.* poor   *c.* better   *d.* different

Da Vinci's Kitchen

In 1981, a book titled *El Codex Romanoff* was discovered at the State Hermitage Museum in Russia. This book contained information on food culture, such as dining etiquette, eating habits, recipes, kitchen management, and new cooking tools. It was confirmed that this book,
5 written in the 1490s, was authored by Leonardo da Vinci.

Cooking was a special hobby for da Vinci, the genius artist, scientist, inventor, and thinker of the Renaissance period. His passion for cooking was more than just a hobby. He worked as a banquet manager on the side for 30 years at Sforza Castle in Italy. He was also a chef in the kitchen and ran
10 a restaurant together with the great painter Botticelli.

As an outstanding inventor, he designed many kitchen tools. Looking at his designs for a pasta-making machine, a boiled-egg slicer, a fork, a napkin dryer, a garlic crusher, and a pepper grinder, one can see the similarities of these designs to the tools used nowadays.

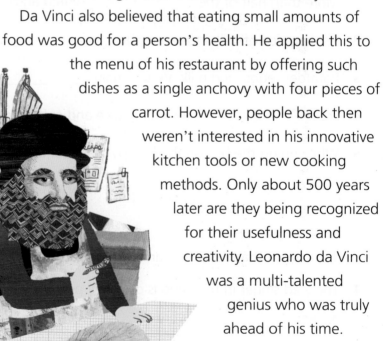

Da Vinci also believed that eating small amounts of food was good for a person's health. He applied this to the menu of his restaurant by offering such dishes as a single anchovy with four pieces of carrot. However, people back then weren't interested in his innovative kitchen tools or new cooking methods. Only about 500 years later are they being recognized for their usefulness and creativity. Leonardo da Vinci was a multi-talented genius who was truly ahead of his time.

1 What is the best title for the passage?

a. The Greatest Inventions of da Vinci

b. An Amazing Book Written by da Vinci

c. A Food Culture Renaissance Led by da Vinci

d. Da Vinci's Surprising Enthusiasm for Cooking

2 What information was NOT contained in *El Codex Romanoff*?

a. How to behave when eating

b. How to cook

c. How to write recipes

d. How to manage a kitchen

3 What does the underlined sentence mean?

a. He cooked only for pleasure.

b. He had a great interest in cooking.

c. He cooked as well as professional chefs.

d. His cooking was at the level of an amateur.

4 What did da Vinci believe was important for a healthy diet?

_____

5 What can be inferred about da Vinci?

a. His primary job was concerned with cooking.

b. His work related to cooking wasn't appreciated in his time.

c. His book about a healthy diet was well known at that time.

d. His dishes tasted so bad that people weren't interested in them.

6 Write T if the statement is true or F if it's false.

1) Da Vinci was once hired in a restaurant managed by a famous artist.

2) Da Vinci designed many kinds of kitchen tools comparable to modern ones.

STRATEGIC SUMMARY

Fill in the blanks with the correct words.

A book written by Leonardo da Vinci was _____ in a Russian museum. Surprisingly, it concerned kitchen etiquette, _____ , and cooking tools. Apparently, da Vinci was very _____ in cooking. He worked as both a banquet manager and a chef. He personally _____ many cooking tools similar to ones used today. Da Vinci believed that eating small amounts of food was the key to a healthy diet. However, his ideas weren't _____ at that time and are only now being appreciated.

recipes	popular	genius	interested	designed	discovered

★ *EXPANDING KNOWLEDGE* ★

Scientists have recently discovered a diet that can help us lose weight and feel better. It is based on Leonardo da Vinci's Mediterranean diet. Essentially, each meal should include one part whole grains, two parts protein, and three parts vegetables. The diet is especially healthy because it includes good fats such as omega-3, which is found in olive oil and fish. The study also found that drinking a glass of wine each day can help lower blood pressure. The popularity of the da Vinci diet shows that many of the health trends followed in the time of da Vinci remain popular today.

1 What is the passage mainly about?

 a. What da Vinci did to keep in shape
 b. Features of da Vinci's diet and how they still work
 c. The importance of eating three meals and exercising
 d. What scientists have found out about da Vinci through the study

2 Write T if the statement is true or F if it's false.

 1) Drinking a glass of wine a day is good for people with low blood pressure.
 2) Many of the health trends in da Vinci's time have remained in fashion.

VOCABULARY REVIEW

A Write the correct word next to its definition.

grain	confirm	apply	passion	grinder

1 the seeds of crops such as wheat or rice: _____

2 to use something in a particular situation: _____

3 a strong desire or enthusiasm for something: _____

4 a machine used for crushing a solid substance into very small pieces: _____

B Complete each sentence with a word in the box. (Change the form if needed.)

similarity	remain	banquet	innovative	trend	appreciate

1 The scientist was _____ for his useful inventions.

2 Their wedding _____ will be held tonight in a nearby hotel.

3 We must develop _____ technology to maintain our leading position.

4 She tries to follow the latest fashion _____ that are quickly changing.

5 I found that there are a lot of _____ between her writing style and mine.

C Find the word that has a similar meaning to the underlined word.

1 The main actor's performance in the play was <u>outstanding</u>.

　　a. ordinary　　　*b.* strange　　　*c.* remarkable　　　*d.* disappointing

2 She has <u>authored</u> a series of fantasy novels.

　　a. read　　　*b.* written　　　*c.* followed　　　*d.* recognized

Before Reading
Have you ever heard a song repeatedly in your head all day?

Earworms

One morning, you turn on the radio and hear your favorite band singing their latest song. On the bus to school, you can still hear it in your head. Even in class, you keep hearing it again and again. Why is
5 this happening? According to experts, you've been infected with an earworm.

(①) You might imagine some strange creature crawling inside your ear. (②) But in reality, an earworm is a part of a song that gets into your head and causes a kind of "itch" on your
10 brain. (③) When you get an earworm, a section of your brain called the *auditory cortex tries to fill in the rest of the song. (④) And once you start "scratching," it is hard to stop. No one is sure exactly what causes earworms. Some think it's like trying to stop a thought. For example, if someone tells you not to think about pink elephants, you will find it is impossible not to.
15 It could work the same way with songs. Others think that an earworm is a simple way to keep the brain busy when it has nothing to do.

What kinds of songs are most likely to cause earworms? Everyone is different, but the songs usually have simple melodies and repetitive lyrics. It doesn't even have to be a real song. Commercials or even cellphone ringtones can cause earworms, too.

You don't have to worry about earworms even if you get one. In fact, you listen to music with not only your ears but also your brain, which is perfectly natural. So just enjoy the music!

*auditory cortex: area of the brain that receives hearing information

1 **What is the best title for the passage?**

   a. The Symptoms of Ear Trouble
   b. How Music Gets Stuck in Your Head
   c. How to Get Rid of Worms in Your Ears
   d. The Songs That Frequently Cause Earworms

2 **How does the writer introduce the topic?**

   a. By explaining an expert's theory
   b. By criticizing the education system
   c. By describing an everyday situation
   d. By analyzing a natural phenomenon

3 **Where would the following sentence best fit?**

So your brain keeps "singing" long after the song has ended.

   a. ①   b. ②   c. ③   d. ④

4 **What does the underlined sentence mean?**

   a. It is impossible not to think about pink elephants.
   b. You are likely to listen to the same songs every day.
   c. The more you try to forget a song, the more you remember it.
   d. Some songs are more likely to get stuck in your head than others.

5 **What features do songs that cause earworms have in common?**

   _____

6 **Write T if the statement is true or F if it's false.**

   1) There are accepted theories that explain why earworms occur.
   2) Some people think that the brain makes earworms when it's idling.

Fill in the blanks with the correct words.

Have you ever had a song _____ in your head over and over again? Experts refer to this as an "earworm." It's not an actual _____. It's part of a song that gets _____ in your auditory cortex and won't go away. No one is sure why this _____, but it usually occurs with songs that have _____ melodies and repetitive lyrics. If you get an earworm, simply try to enjoy the song while it is in your head.

worm	simple	repeat	infected	happens	stuck

★ EXPANDING KNOWLEDGE ★

When you put a large seashell up to your ear, you may hear a sound like rolling waves. Have you ever wondered how seashells make the sound of the ocean? The truth is they don't. The noises may sound like the roar of the ocean, but they are actually just the small sounds that are around you all the time. How does this happen? It has to do with the shape of the shell. The inside of a shell is hollow, just like that of a guitar. And also like a guitar, this empty area makes sounds much louder. So whenever you hold a shell up to your ear, you're really hearing all the little noises around you being made louder by the shell.

1 What is the best pair for blanks (A) and (B)?

> The reason we hear the ocean roar in a seashell is that the _____(A)_____ area inside of a shell makes _____(B)_____.

      (A)   (B)

a. round — little noises louder
b. deep — sounds much clearer
c. empty — small sounds louder
d. hollow — your hearing better

2 Write T if the statement is true or F if it's false.

1) The noises from the seashell sound like the roar of ocean waves.
2) The sounds you hear in a seashell are the sounds that are always being made around you.

VOCABULARY REVIEW

A Write the correct word next to its definition.

itch	roar	crawl	rest	phenomenon

1 to move slowly near the ground: _____

2 the remaining part of something: _____

3 an uncomfortable feeling that encourages scratching the skin: _____

4 a loud noise made by something such as the wind or an animal: _____

B Complete each sentence with a word in the box. (Change the form if needed.)

lyric	infect	shape	wonder	commercial	repetitive

1 Two people were _____ with the Ebola virus in the U.S.

2 The new opera house is designed in the _____ of a flower.

3 I _____ where my childhood friend Jane is now and if she is okay.

4 The students felt bored after performing _____ tasks for a long time.

5 These beautiful _____ were written by David, who is a famous songwriter.

C Find the word that has a similar meaning to the underlined word.

1 The skunk lives in a <u>hollow</u> log in the forest.

    a. thick   *b.* empty   *c.* heavy   *d.* delicious

2 I'm sure Emma's weird behavior <u>has to do with</u> the letter she received.

    a. is similar to   *b.* is related to

    c. is considered as   *d.* is covered with

Before Reading
Whose eyesight do you think is better,
a human's or a dog's?

Dog Vision

Have you ever wondered how the world looks to a dog? Perhaps shoes look like fun toys, and bones resemble delicious meals. Actually, there are some big differences between human vision and dog vision.

5 Humans rely on their vision for nearly everything they do, but dogs are different. (①) They can hear and smell extremely well. (②) In fact, human vision is five times better than dog vision. (③) Dogs also distinguish fewer colors than we do. (④) They cannot tell green from blue or red from yellow. To a dog, the world is mostly shades of blue and yellow. Another big difference is that our eyes face forward, while a dog's eyes are on either side

10 of its head. Because of this, dogs have much poorer depth perception. This means they cannot easily tell _____(A)_____ objects are.

However, dogs do have some advantages when it comes to vision. For one thing, the position of their eyes helps them see more of their surroundings, not just what is directly in front of them. Moreover, dogs

15 have a special surface in the back of their eyes that lets them see in the dark much better than we can. And they are also a lot better at seeing movement far away. All of these features help make dogs excellent hunters.

When you think about it, it is not really fair to say that humans see better than dogs. It is more accurate to say that dogs simply see things differently than we do.

1 What is the passage mainly about?

a. How to improve your dog's eyesight

b. How hunting dogs are different from pet dogs

c. How dogs see the world compared to humans

d. The differences between the human body and a dog's body

2 Where would the following sentence best fit?

Therefore, their vision doesn't need to be as good as ours.

a. ①   b. ②   c. ③   d. ④

3 What is the best choice for blank (A)?

a. what colors

b. what shapes

c. how big or small

d. how close or far away

4 How does the position of the eyes help dogs?

_____

5 A dog's eyes are NOT superior to a human's at _____.

a. discriminating between colors

b. seeing things that are not in front of them

c. seeing in low lighting

d. detecting the motion of an object

6 Write T if the statement is true or F if it's false.

1) The position of dogs' eyes has its advantages and disadvantages.

2) The reason dogs can be good hunters is completely unrelated to their vision.

Fill in the blanks with the correct words.

Dogs' Eyes

Features
- Positioned on the _____ of their head
- Limited in seeing a range of _____ and depth

Advantages
- Can see a greater area around them due to their eye _____
- Have a special _____ in the back of their eyes that gives them good night vision
- Are good at seeing things in the _____

positioning   distance   colors   surface   sides   vision

★ EXPANDING KNOWLEDGE ★

Imagine your dog were running toward you from across the street. You may think he would recognize you based solely on your appearance. But that's not true. The truth is that dogs cannot see motionless objects very well. So how does your dog know it is you? He can recognize you based on your unique gestures, in addition to your smell or voice. As a matter of fact, a dog's vision is very _____(A)_____ to motion. Even the smallest change in your posture means a lot to your dog. This is important to keep in mind when training your dog. If you want your dog to act without spoken commands, you must always use the same gestures to allow your dog to understand.

1 What is the passage mainly about?

a. How to train your dog effectively

b. How your dog can recognize you

c. How to make your dog's vision better

d. How a dog responds to even the smallest motion

2 What is the best choice for blank (A)?

a. dull   b. superior   c. terrible   d. sensitive

Unit · 13
VOCABULARY REVIEW

A Write the correct word next to its definition.

appearance	vision	depth	surface	directly

1 the ability to see: _____

2 the top part or outside of something: _____

3 exactly in a particular position or way: _____

4 the distance from the top to the bottom of something: _____

B Complete each sentence with a word in the box. (Change the form if needed.)

tell	gesture	surroundings	sensitive	command	motionless

1 It's hard to _____ the difference between a cold and the flu.

2 The soldier thought the _____ from his captain weren't rational.

3 Robert is very _____ to the cold, so he wears a thick coat these days.

4 Some worms blend in with their _____ so that it's difficult to see them.

5 Amy was so shocked by the news that she sat _____ for five minutes.

C Find the word that has a similar meaning to the underlined word.

1 You should keep in mind that you only have ten minutes to present your idea.

  a. hope   *b.* recognize   *c.* promise   *d.* remember

2 She started to play golf solely for fun, but she later became a professional.

  a. only   *b.* partly   *c.* even   *d.* sometimes

Give Me a Hug!

A few years ago, a man stood in the busiest street in Sydney offering free hugs to strangers. Someone made a video of this and put it online, and it soon became a worldwide sensation. If you get a chance to watch this video clip, one thing will really stand out to you — the huggers all have big smiles.
5 Hugging makes us feel better, and now scientists have proven why.

One reason is that hugging actually has a direct impact on our emotions. (①) For a start, the act of hugging releases pleasurable chemicals like dopamine into our brain. (②) In addition, a study led by Dr. Karen Grewen at the University of North Carolina found that hugging causes the
10 body to produce more oxytocin. (③) So higher levels of oxytocin make us more loving towards other people. (④) Perhaps this is why couples enjoy hugging so much.

Besides activating the chemicals related to our feelings, hugging is good for _____(A)_____. Higher oxytocin levels are also concerned with
15 physical health, particularly of the heart. For example, another study led by Grewen found that hugging leads to decreased blood pressure, less stress, and a lower risk of heart disease.

This research suggests that people should hug more often than they do these days. Hugs shouldn't just be saved for partners and small children.
20 Instead, people should be more willing to hug friends, family members, and even their workmates and neighbors.
That way, everyone can enjoy the
mental and physical benefits
of hugging!

1 What is the passage mainly about?

    a. What causes people to hug each other
    b. Who people usually hug in their daily life
    c. What benefits people can get from hugging
    d. Why "free hugs" created a worldwide sensation

2 Where would the following sentence best fit?

> It is a chemical that is associated with caring and bonding.

    a. ①   *b.* ②   *c.* ③   *d.* ④

3 What is the best choice for blank (A)?

    a. our minds
    b. our bodies
    c. our thoughts
    d. our emotions

4 According to Grewen's research, how does hugging help us physically?

_____

5 What does the underlined sentence mean?

    a. We should hug young children more often than others.
    b. We should share the benefits of hugging with everyone.
    c. The health benefits of hugging differ based on relationships.
    d. It is important to have a good relationship with family members.

6 What is NOT mentioned as an effect of hugging?

    a. It makes us feel pleasure.
    b. It can be helpful for relationships.
    c. It helps us relieve stress by lowering oxytocin levels.
    d. It reduces the risk of heart disease.

Fill in the blanks with the correct words.

Hugging is one way that people can make themselves feel better. Scientists have now shown that this is due to the fact that it causes dopamine to be _____ in our brains, which causes feelings of pleasure. It also _____ the production of oxytocin, which makes us _____ about others more. The scientists also found that hugging is good for our physical _____. It decreases blood pressure, reduces stress, and lowers our risk of heart disease. Therefore, they _____ that people hug one another more often.

care   health   pleasure   released   increases   recommend

★ EXPANDING KNOWLEDGE ★

These days, finding free hugs is easy thanks to Juan Mann. Here is his story:

I was standing in the arrivals terminal when I noticed all the other people laughing and hugging their friends and family. I really wanted someone to hug me. So I made a cardboard sign saying "Free Hugs" and took it to the city's busiest street corner. At first, nobody even looked at me. But then a lady came up to me and said her dog just died that morning and that her daughter had died exactly one year before. So I got down on one knee, put my arms around her and gave her a hug. After we parted, the woman was smiling.

1 What can be inferred from the underlined part?

a. She had been happy beforehand.

b. She had a very exciting experience.

c. She thought Juan Mann was very funny.

d. She had been comforted by Juan Mann's hug.

2 Write T if the statement is true or F if it's false.

1) Juan Mann planned the free hugs campaign from the start.

2) At first, no one responded to Mann's offer for free hugs.

VOCABULARY REVIEW

A Write the correct word next to its definition.

part	release	bonding	risk	sensation

1 to separate from each other: _____

2 the chance that something bad may happen: _____

3 a person or thing that causes great interest or excitement: _____

4 the development or creation of a strong relationship with someone: _____

B Complete each sentence with a word in the box. (Change the form if needed.)

mental	get down	stand out	save	suggest	particularly

1 You look terrible. I _____ that you go to see a doctor.

2 Mark _____ on his knees and asked her for forgiveness.

3 I _____ like this photo because it reminds me of where I grew up.

4 I have some money in the bank that I've been _____ for a rainy day.

5 Some studies show that exercise can help people suffering from _____ illness.

C Find the word that has a similar meaning to the underlined word.

1 We want you to have a <u>pleasurable</u> experience at our hotel.

    a. unique   *b.* attractive   *c.* enjoyable   *d.* innovative

2 Twitter has had an <u>impact</u> on the way people communicate with each other.

    a. idea   *b.* effect   *c.* action   *d.* change

FASHION

Full Figured Fashion Week

Do you like to keep current with what's going on in the fashion world? Then you have to attend this year's Full Figured Fashion Week. For decades, the fashion industry has ignored larger, more realistic-looking models. Instead, the most famous fashions are worn by models who are unhealthily skinny. Some models, trying to stay thin, have even died from eating disorders. FFFWeek aims for a return to responsibility in fashion.

FFFWeek was founded by Gwendolyn DeVoe, a former plus-size model. She and her colleagues were
10 tired of being overlooked at the traditional Fashion Week events held in New York, London, Milan, and Paris each year. So in 2009, DeVoe founded FFFWeek. One of her intentions was to encourage support for plus-size clothing designs and the models who wear them.
15 She also wanted to draw attention to the health hazards of traditional fashion modeling. The models working in the industry are not the only ones at risk. In addition, women all over the world see the _____(A)_____ standard of beauty set
20 by skinny models. When they can't reach that standard themselves, women suffer both mentally and physically.

FFFWeek takes place in June in New York City. In addition to fashion shows, there are group
25 discussions and a contest for designers. More than a thousand people attend FFFWeek each year, including representatives from the world's largest fashion companies. With time, FFFWeek is sure to grow, and as it does, it will continue to teach people the truth about the
30 relationship between fashion and health.

1 What is the best title for the passage?

  a. Fashions Causing Health Hazards
  b. Fashion Models with Eating Disorders
  c. Trendy Fashions by Full-Figured Designers
  d. A Special Fashion Week for Plus-Size People

2 Who are full-figured fashion models?

_____

3 Why did Gwendolyn DeVoe found FFFWeek?

  a. She wanted to start fashion shows by herself.
  b. She wanted to hire designers making plus-size clothing.
  c. She didn't want to be disregarded by usual fashion shows anymore.
  d. She didn't want to participate in the fashion shows in Milan and Paris.

4 What is the best choice for blank (A)?

  a. uncertain
  b. unrealistic
  c. unsatisfying
  d. unavoidable

5 What is NOT true according to the passage?

  a. Gwendolyn DeVoe wasn't welcomed by traditional fashion shows.
  b. FFFWeek supports designers who make plus-size outfits.
  c. The standard of beauty inspired by fashion models is harmful to women's health.
  d. The world's largest fashion companies don't support FFFWeek.

6 Write T if the statement is true or F if it's false.

  1) Some models working in the fashion industry go through health problems.
  2) Anyone can attend the group discussions and contest during FFFWeek.

Fill in the blanks with the correct words.

Full Figured Fashion Week	A fashion week for _____ models and clothing designs

Intentions
- To raise health _____ in the fashion industry
- To present a more _____ image of beauty for women

Events
- Fashion shows, group discussions, and a design _____
- _____ by over 1,000 people

> awareness   realistic   contest   attended   plus-size   skinny

★ EXPANDING KNOWLEDGE ★

To be beautiful is to be extremely skinny, according to the fashion industry. That's why many have called for the industry to promote a healthier ideal by regulating the look of their models. The "Size Zero Debate" has gained attention since three models died due to health problems from being too thin. Most models are size-zero, and their *BMI is 16 or lower, which puts them at risk of starvation. In response to this, Madrid began banning models with a BMI under 18. Milan and the U.S. soon followed. _____(A)_____, for the ban to be effective, designers and consumers have to do more. Designers must not use skinny models on runways or for advertisements. And consumers must boycott brands that use unrealistically thin models in their advertising.

*BMI (Body Mass Index): a measure of whether someone is overweight or underweight

1 What is the main claim of the writer?

  a. Advertisers need to use more fashion models in their advertisements.
  b. Designers who are too thin must be expelled from the fashion industry.
  c. The World Health Organization has to set and announce an ideal body image.
  d. Designers and consumers should take action to promote a healthy body image.

2 What is the best choice for blank (A)?

  a. Likewise
  b. Therefore
  c. Otherwise
  d. Nevertheless

VOCABULARY REVIEW

A Write the correct word next to its definition.

| representative | starvation | hazard | former | promote |

1 having had a particular status or position in the past: _____

2 something that can be dangerous or cause problems: _____

3 to help or encourage something to happen, increase, or spread: _____

4 the state of suffering or death caused by not having enough food: _____

B Complete each sentence with a word in the box. (Change the form if needed.)

| responsibility | at risk | boycott | intention | due to | overlook |

1 I want to know your real _____ in coming here.

2 The flight to Paris has been canceled _____ the storm.

3 He was _____ for employment because of his disability.

4 People who drink water from this dirty river are _____ of getting sick.

5 People _____ the company's products after a bug was found in one of its snacks.

C Find the word that has a similar meaning to the underlined word.

1 I want to be <u>skinny</u> but I also want to be healthy.

   a. very pretty   *b.* very tall   *c.* very thin   *d.* very pale

2 Zachary is suffering from a mental <u>disorder</u> that causes him to be unhappy.

   a. health   *b.* stress   *c.* disease   *d.* power

The Mother Teresa Effect

When was the last time you helped another person? Maybe you helped an elderly person up some stairs or made a donation to a charity. Do you remember how this act of kindness made you

5 feel? Research suggests that helping others can make us feel better and can even improve our physical health. This phenomenon is known as the Mother Teresa Effect.

The term originated from a study conducted

10 at Harvard University. ① Researchers showed 132 students a film about the work of Mother Teresa, a Catholic nun who helped the poor and sick of 20th-century Calcutta, India. ② Mother Teresa said that happiness can't be found without prayer. ③ When the film finished, the researchers measured the students' levels of immunoglobulin A, which is

15 one of the body's first defenses against viruses. ④ Amazingly, their levels of immunoglobulin A had increased significantly after simply watching Mother Teresa doing charity work.

So, if watching someone performing acts of charity has such a strong effect on people, what are the effects of actually doing charity work yourself? A study of 3,000 volunteers conducted by Allan Luks and Penny Payne found a variety of psychological and physical benefits. The volunteers experienced a feeling of happiness and energy followed by a "helper's high" of peace and calm. Physically, the

25 volunteers found that some of their health problems, such as stress, chronic pain, and insomnia, were _____(A)_____ after volunteering.

All this evidence shows that helping others has a positive influence on not only our minds but also our

30 health. Helping others also means helping ourselves, so why not give it a try?

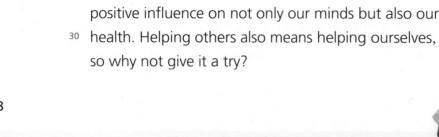

1 What is the passage mainly about?

  a. The scientific facts behind a helper's high
  b. A close relationship between feelings and health
  c. The psychological and physical benefits of helping others
  d. How Mother Teresa dedicated herself to helping poor people

2 Which sentence is NOT needed in the passage?

  a. ①   *b.* ②   *c.* ③   *d.* ④

3 According to the 2nd paragraph, we can improve our physical health by

_____.

  a. helping other students
  b. watching a great movie
  c. watching someone do charity work
  d. trying to strengthen our immune systems

4 What psychological benefit can people get by helping others?

_____

5 What is the best choice for blank (A)?

  a. reduced
  b. increased
  c. worsened
  d. continued

6 Write T if the statement is true or F if it's false.

  1) The term "Mother Teresa Effect" was invented by people who worked with Mother Teresa.
  2) Scientific research found that we feel better when we help others.

Fill in the blanks with the correct words.

The Mother Teresa Effect	The phenomenon that _____ others makes us happy and healthy

An experiment at Harvard University
• A(n) _____ in immunoglobulin A after witnessing someone do _____ work

The effects of doing volunteer work
• Positive emotions, such as _____, as well as a "helper's high" of calm and peace
• Relief from _____ problems, such as stress, insomnia, and pain

> helping   health   charity   benefits   increase   happiness

★ EXPANDING KNOWLEDGE ★

Mother Teresa was born in Albania. At age eighteen, she joined a religious order and became a nun. A few years later, she moved to India and decided to dedicate her whole life to the welfare of the poor. On October 7, 1950, Mother Teresa began the Missionaries of Charity to help the poor, sick, and orphaned. It became the center of all her activities with its branches spread to many parts of the country. Today, the Missionaries of Charity helps the poor in several countries in Asia, Africa, Eastern Europe, and Latin America. In these places, the organization provides relief from natural disasters and cares for alcoholics, the homeless, and AIDS sufferers.

1 What is NOT mentioned about Mother Teresa?

a. When she became a nun

b. Where she helped the poor

c. What organization she founded

d. What activities she did worldwide

2 Write T if the statement is true or F if it's false.

1) Mother Teresa helped people in need for most of her life.

2) The organization established by Mother Teresa is no longer active.

VOCABULARY REVIEW

A Write the correct word next to its definition.

relief	chronic	welfare	defense	dedicate

1 the health and happiness of a person: _____

2 to give all your time and effort to something: _____

3 lasting a long time and difficult to cure or fix: _____

4 food, money, or services given to people in need: _____

B Complete each sentence with a word in the box. (Change the form if needed.)

donation	branch	prayer	disaster	measure	volunteer

1 Last month's floods were a horrible natural _____.

2 He made a big _____ to a charity for people in need.

3 We are recruiting a few _____ to help organize school fundraisers.

4 Recently, Amanda expanded her business by opening a new _____.

5 The policeman stopped the car to _____ the driver's blood alcohol level.

C Find the word that has a similar meaning to the underlined word.

1 They are <u>conducting</u> research into the causes of the disease.

    a. coming by   *b.* putting off   *c.* carrying out   *d.* figuring out

2 The relationship between blood types and personalities lacks scientific <u>evidence</u>.

    a. theory   *b.* proof   *c.* method   *d.* comment

Before Reading
How would Earth be different if there were no moon?

The Moon

People enjoy gazing at the moon on a clear night. It has inspired art, shaped mythology, and influenced language. Furthermore, the movements of the moon play an essential role in making Earth habitable. So what would life be like if the moon didn't exist?

5 Obviously, there would be no lunar or solar eclipses if there were no moon. But this is just the beginning. Without the moon, our planet would spin much faster because the moon's *gravitational pull on Earth's oceans slows its rotation. Before the formation of the moon billions of years ago, days were only 10 hours long. Our days would still be this short without the

10 moon.

If Earth rotated this quickly, the winds would be much stronger. (①) Consider the gas giant Jupiter, which spins much faster than Earth. (②) And they last centuries and stretch across the entire planet. (③) These strong storms are what cause Jupiter's banded appearance. (④) If the

15 moon did not exist, Earth might have similar weather.

Life would be _____(A)_____ if the winds on Earth were this strong. Try to picture walking down the street or talking with a friend with constantly howling winds. Air and sea travel would be nearly impossible, thus preventing the exchange of

20 ideas and technologies. It is even probable that some life forms would never come to exist!

Our closest neighbor in space has played a major role in shaping our planet. So the next time you look at the moon, think of the role it has played

25 and how different our planet would be without it!

*gravitational: related to the force of gravity

1 What is the passage mainly about?

    a. Life on the moon

    b. Life without the moon

    c. The mystery of the moon

    d. The moon in human culture

2 How does the moon slow down the speed at which Earth spins?

_____

3 Where would the following sentence best fit?

> Its windstorms are enormous — many times larger than those on Earth.

    a. ①   *b.* ②   *c.* ③   *d.* ④

4 Why does the writer mention Jupiter?

    a. To predict a weather change on the moon

    b. To compare the size of the moon and Earth

    c. To give an example of a planet without moons

    d. To explain how the rotation speed affects the weather

5 What is the best choice for blank (A)?

    a. improved   *b.* enhanced

    c. restricted   *d.* accelerated

6 What is NOT mentioned as a possible effect of Earth having no moon?

    a. Lunar or solar eclipses would not occur.

    b. The days would be much shorter than now.

    c. Wind speeds would increase greatly.

    d. New living things would appear in various forms.

Fill in the blanks with the correct words.

What If There Were No Moon?

Possible effects
- Lunar and solar _____ could not happen.
- Earth's days would be _____ — just 10 hours long.
- Bad weather, like windstorms, might occur.
  → Earth's weather might be _____ to Jupiter's.
- Life would be affected.
  → Some life forms might become _____.

| shorter | rotation | extinct | eclipses | similar |

★ EXPANDING KNOWLEDGE ★

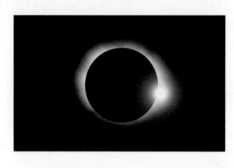

People have watched the moon for thousands of years. Its continuous presence has made it the subject of stories and legends in every culture of the world. For example, South African Bushmen explain lunar eclipses with the story of a lion covering the moon with its paw to be able to hunt in the dark. In many cultures, the moon has often acted as a symbol of change, death, and rebirth. There are plenty of superstitions involving the moon, too. In medieval Europe, sleeping under the moonlight was thought to drive people mad; this is the origin of the word "lunatic," based on the Latin word for the moon. Of course, we've all heard about people transforming into werewolves when the moon is full. Clearly, the moon occupies a central place in people's imagination, _____(A)_____ their cultural background.

1 What is the purpose of the passage?

a. To describe the regular changes of the moon
b. To prove some superstitions about the moon
c. To explain the origin of a Latin word for the moon
d. To explain the symbolic meanings of the moon in stories

2 What is the best choice for blank (A)?

a. due to   b. along with   c. regardless of   d. according to

VOCABULARY REVIEW

A Write the correct word next to its definition.

rotate	transform	stretch	probable	habitable

1 likely to happen or be true: _____

2 suitable for people to live in: _____

3 to turn in a circle around an axis: _____

4 to completely change the appearance of something: _____

B Complete each sentence with a word in the box. (Change the form if needed.)

legend	spin	gaze at	inspire	presence	medieval

1 Have you ever felt the _____ of a ghost?

2 Earth _____ in a circle as it travels around the sun.

3 He _____ the picture and thought about its meaning.

4 There are many _____ about the fall of this ancient city.

5 This book describes the Christian world's view of _____ times at around 1200 AD.

C Find the word that has a similar meaning to the underlined word.

1 Bullying has an <u>enormous</u> impact on children that are targets of it.

    a. negative   *b.* huge   *c.* direct   *d.* potential

2 As a child, I <u>pictured</u> myself growing up to become a writer.

    a. recorded   *b.* hoped   *c.* imagined   *d.* remembered

Piri's Map

In 1929, historians working in Turkey found an old map.
It was made in 1513 by a Turkish admiral named Piri.
This map interested people because it was one of the
oldest maps to show America. However, because
5 the map does not have the lines of *latitude and
*longitude that most maps use today, people
thought it was inaccurate.

However, this changed in 1953. ① A researcher
discovered that the map uses many circular points to
10 show location. ② When he transferred the map onto a
grid and onto a globe, he found it totally accurate. ③ In fact, the map was
so accurate that the U.S. Air Force used it to correct mistakes in their own
maps. ④ Soon they admitted their mistakes and stopped using Piri's map.

Another surprise is that the map includes Antarctica. Antarctica was
not discovered until 1820, 300 years after the map was
made. But an even greater mystery is that it accurately
shows the Antarctic coastline. According to experts,
Antarctica has been covered by ice for more than 6,000
years. So how was Piri able to draw the land under the
ice?

In fact, Piri consulted many other ancient maps to
draw his own. Some believe that ancient civilizations
discovered and mapped Antarctica before it was
covered with ice. As to its accuracy, others even argue
that Piri received the help of aliens from outer space.
But until we find more evidence, it seems Piri's map
will remain a mystery.

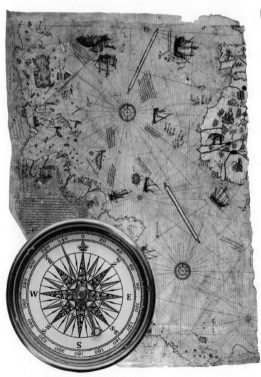

*latitude: horizontal lines on a map or a globe
*longitude: vertical lines on a map or a globe

1 What is the passage mainly about?

a. The mysteries of Piri's map

b. When Antarctica was discovered

c. The historical meaning of Piri's map

d. Proof of the existence of aliens in the universe

2 Why did Piri's map first interest people when it was discovered?

_____

3 Why did people think Piri's map was inaccurate?

a. Because it didn't have many circular points.

b. Because it didn't follow today's mapping system.

c. Because it was one of the oldest maps ever found.

d. Because Piri used many other ancient maps to draw it.

4 Which sentence is NOT needed in the passage?

a. ①   b. ②   c. ③   d. ④

5 Why is Piri's map surprising? (Choose two.)

a. Because it's very accurate.

b. Because it shows the coastline of Antarctica.

c. Because it was drawn with the help of aliens.

d. Because it has lines of latitude and longitude.

6 Write T if the statement is true or F if it's false.

1) Piri's map was found by a Turkish admiral in 1929.

2) Piri's map was made before Antarctica was discovered.

Fill in the blanks with the correct words.

Piri's Map — A map _____ in 1513 by the Turkish admiral Piri

Mysterious features
- _____ enough to correct errors in U.S. Air Force maps
- Shows the Antarctic _____, which is covered by ice

Suggested explanations
- Piri used old maps drawn by ancient _____.
- _____ from outer space helped Piri make his map.

large   drawn   accurate   coastline   creatures   civilizations

★ EXPANDING KNOWLEDGE ★

Piri Reis was born between 1465 and 1470 in Gallipoli, Turkey. He joined the navy of the Ottoman Empire at an early age, and spent many years fighting at sea. He returned home to Gallipoli in 1511 and began writing down the things he had learned. In 1513, he produced an amazingly accurate map of the world. Then, in 1521, he finished writing his *Book of Navigation*. The book contained 290 maps and gave lots of information, including the technique of using a compass and methods of finding directions using the stars. Despite these important contributions, he was executed for refusing to go to war again when he was around 90.

1 What is the passage mainly about?

a. The unjust death of Piri Reis
b. The accuracy of the Piri Reis map
c. The power of the Ottoman Empire
d. The biography and achievements of Piri Reis

2 Write T if the statement is true or F if it's false.

1) Piri Reis produced a world map during sea battles.
2) Piri Reis was killed during a war when he was about 90 years old.

A Write the correct word next to its definition.

alien	globe	compass	admiral	civilization

1 an officer who leads a navy: _____

2 a creature from a different planet: _____

3 a ball-shaped object with a map of the world drawn on it: _____

4 a device used to find directions with a needle pointing north: _____

B Complete each sentence with a word in the box. (Change the form if needed.)

contribution	correct	expert	admit	execute	empire

1 If you have a bad habit, you should try to _____ it.

2 After the war, many people were _____ for war crimes.

3 I don't like David, but I _____ that he is a professional at work.

4 He is known as a(n) _____ in the field of computer programming.

5 Darwin made a significant _____ to our understanding of evolution.

C Find the word that has a similar meaning to the underlined word.

1 Many people <u>argue</u> that this knife was used in ancient times.

   a. claim   *b.* reach   *c.* refuse   *d.* develop

2 This clock is <u>accurate</u> to a hundredth of a second.

   a. quick   *b.* exact   *c.* ancient   *d.* suitable

Claude Monet

In 1912, at the age of 72, the great French Impressionist painter Claude Monet found out that he had *cataracts. "I no longer saw colors with the same intensity," he once told a friend. "The reds seemed dark to me, the pinks were unexciting, and the mixed colors and lower tones escaped me
5 completely."

Monet's later artwork is much different in style from his early pieces. It is more abstract, and the vibrant colors are gone. Why did this happen? Eye doctor and art lover Michael Marmor has a theory. He argues that Monet's vision caused him to see most colors in shades of yellow and brown. Based
10 on this, Professor Marmor recreated Monet's paintings as ① he probably would have seen them. ② His works show Monet's paintings as blurry and dull. If this is how Monet really saw ③ his work, it may explain why ④ he used more blues as he got older: to compensate for his yellowed vision.

_____(A)_____ Professor Marmor's work, not all art scholars are convinced that Monet changed his style because of his condition. One critic argues that Monet's paintings before and after his surgery to remove his cataracts look similar. Others insist that Monet was a master painter and that any changes
20 in his art style would have been intentional. Although there are many hypotheses that attempt to explain the change in Monet's work, what we know for sure is that Monet's art continues to inspire, despite the difficulties he faced.

*cataract: an eye disease that causes cloudy, poor eyesight

1 What is the passage mainly about?

   a. What caused the change in Monet's work

   b. The characteristics of Monet's later artwork

   c. Monet's inspiration to overcome his hardship

   d. Why Monet's later work isn't as good as his early work

2 What are the features of Monet's later work?

_____

3 What does NOT refer to the same person?

   a. ①   *b.* ②   *c.* ③   *d.* ④

4 What is the best choice for blank (A)?

   a. In spite of   *b.* Because of

   c. According to   *d.* In addition to

5 What is NOT true about Monet's vision?

   a. His eye disease had had an impact on his vision.

   b. He had difficulty distinguishing colors.

   c. He confessed his eye problems and the effect they had.

   d. His medical treatment clearly improved his vision and artwork.

6 Write T if the statement is true or F if it's false.

   1) Some people don't agree with Marmor's opinion and think the change was intended.

   2) The change in Monet's later work decreased his influence on the art world.

Fill in the blanks with the correct words.

In his 70s, Claude Monet discovered he had cataracts. This condition affected the great artist's _____. He even admitted to a friend that he saw colors _____. One expert thinks this might have led to the change in Monet's style during his later years. His later artwork is more abstract and _____ the bright colors of his earlier paintings. However, other experts _____ with this theory. They believe this was a(n) _____ change in style by Monet.

> intentional   lacks   disagree   differently   vision   surgery

★ EXPANDING KNOWLEDGE ★

Impressionism is the name given to a style of painting, but where did the name come from? In 1872, the French painter Claude Monet drew a painting titled *Impression*, *Sunrise*, which shows sunlight dancing on the surface of water. From then on, Monet used the name Impressionism to refer to his style of art. The light, the color, and the energetic qualities of nature were emphasized by the Impressionist movement. Painters like Degas and Pissarro joined Monet in capturing these fleeting, joyous moments of natural beauty in their paintings. The movement that they created lasted from 1870 to 1910 and affected the art world in ways that can still be felt today.

1 What is NOT mentioned about Impressionism in the passage?

   a. How the name was created

   b. Who participated in the movement

   c. How long it lasted

   d. How it has changed in modern days

2 What were some features of the Impressionist movement?

_____

Unit ★ 19
VOCABULARY REVIEW

A Write the correct word next to its definition.

emphasize	blurry	convinced	compensate	inspire

1 difficult to see something clearly: _____

2 to motivate someone to do something: _____

3 completely certain that something is true: _____

4 to give special importance or attention to something: _____

B Complete each sentence with a word in the box. (Change the form if needed.)

theory	surgery	abstract	fleeting	energetic	attempt

1 There is no scientific evidence to support this _____.

2 I'm particularly interested in both modern and _____ art.

3 He had multiple _____ on his leg after the serious car accident.

4 Amy got a(n) _____ look at the famous building as she drove by it.

5 David is a smart and _____ young man with a passion for dancing.

C Find the word that has a similar meaning to the underlined word.

1 We didn't get to see all of the great <u>pieces</u> of art in the big museum.

    a. parts   *b.* works   *c.* techniques   *d.* types

2 The company <u>faced</u> a financial crisis after launching the product.

    a. encountered   *b.* disliked   *c.* bothered   *d.* called

New Medicine

If you are sick or hurt, a visit to your doctor could make you feel better. But there is one thing that almost no one likes at the doctor's office: getting a shot.

5   But now scientists have invented something that might eventually replace shots, along with many other kinds of medicine and pills. (①) It is a special microchip, as thin as paper and about the

10 size of a small coin. (②) Doctors simply place medicine inside special pockets located in the microchip. (③) Once it's inside, the microchip releases just as much medicine as you need, exactly when you need it. (④)

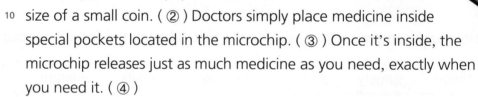

_____(A)_____ Each pocket is sealed with

15 different kinds of material called polymers. These various polymers begin to break down at different speeds when they are inside the human body. Once they completely break down, the medicine is released. This allows doctors to control the timing.

Besides helping you avoid painful shots, there are a couple of

20 important advantages to this new technology. For one thing, patients don't have to worry about remembering when to take their medicine; the chip remembers for them. It is also helpful for travelers who need several shots to protect themselves against a possible disease, and it saves them repeated trips to the doctor's office.

The microchips can keep providing medicine for up to five months. After that, they safely melt away into your body. It sounds a lot better than a sharp needle in the arm, doesn't it?

1 What is the passage mainly about?

a. New technology could replace getting a shot.

b. Getting a shot is the best way to cure a disease.

c. Various kinds of packaged medicine are being developed.

d. New equipment could reduce the cost of taking medicine.

2 Where would the following sentence best fit?

> Then they put the microchip into your body.

a. ①　　　　　b. ②　　　　　c. ③　　　　　d. ④

3 What is the best choice for blank (A)?

a. Why is it needed?

b. How does it do this?

c. When can it be used?

d. What does it consist of?

4 What do the polymers do to control the timing of releasing the medicine inside the human body?

_____

5 For whom is the microchip NOT useful?

a. Bruce, who is afraid to get a shot in his arm

b. Leslie, who will undergo an operation on her eyes

c. James, who needs to take medicine three times a day

d. Emily, who wants to receive vaccines before leaving for Africa

6 Write T if the statement is true or F if it's false.

1) The microchip reminds the patients to take medicine at exact times.

2) The microchip has to be removed after five months.

Fill in the blanks with the correct words.

The New Microchip	A new way of providing medicine to patients

How to use it
- Doctors put medicine _____ a microchip.
- It is _____ into the patient's body.

Advantages
- It can replace _____ shots.
- It automatically releases medicine in a(n) _____ manner, so patients don't need to remember.
- It saves _____ visits to the doctor's office in the case of certain vaccinations.

> inside   painful   implanted   repeated   timely   disease

★ EXPANDING KNOWLEDGE ★

Like humans, dogs sometimes need medicine to get over an illness. _____(A)_____, use the following technique. First, press your dog's lips to show the teeth and open your dog's mouth. Now, place the pill in the middle of the back of your dog's tongue. If the pill is too far forward or to the side, your dog will spit it out. Then rub your dog's throat to help him or her swallow the pill. Alternatively, you can hide medicine in your dog's food. Whatever you do, never crush the pill. The unpleasant taste of the medicine powder will make it harder for your dog to swallow it and may make the strategy less effective.

1 What is the best choice for blank (A)?

- *a.* To give your dog a pill
- *b.* To hide your dog's pills
- *c.* To feed your dog easily
- *d.* To treat your dog like a person

2 Write T if the statement is true or F if it's false.

- *1)* You need to put the pill in the middle of the front of your dog's tongue.
- *2)* Crushing a pill into powder is not a proper way to medicate your dog.

VOCABULARY REVIEW

A Write the correct word next to its definition.

shot	place	illness	swallow	melt away

1 to disappear slowly: _____

2 to put something somewhere: _____

3 a state of feeling sick or of having a disease: _____

4 to make food or drink move from your mouth into your stomach: _____

B Complete each sentence with a word in the box. (Change the form if needed.)

seal	avoid	up to	get over	technique	along with

1 It took a long time for me to _____ this serious flu.

2 Using flashcards is a basic _____ for memorizing vocabulary.

3 We have four meeting rooms, which can hold _____ 50 people.

4 To store homemade jam properly, you need to _____ the jar tightly.

5 People often _____ making a decision because they're afraid of making the wrong one.

C Find the word that has a similar meaning to the underlined word.

1 The environmental <u>advantages</u> of recycling are often overlooked.

    a. benefits   *b.* resources   *c.* costs   *d.* efforts

2 We can spend the weekend on the beach or, <u>alternatively</u>, go hiking in the mountains.

    a. surely   *b.* instead   *c.* probably   *d.* unfortunately

MEMO

Reading FORWARD

ADVANCED 1

★ *Word Book* ★

Unit ★ 11 PEOPLE

reserve	동	남겨두다, 보존하다
promote	동	촉진하다; 홍보하다
superior	형	우수한, 우월한
consistency	명	일관성

innovative	형	혁신적인
recognize	동	알아보다; 인정하다
multi-talented	형	다재다능한
enthusiasm	명	열정, 열의
behave	동	행동하다; 예의 바르게 행동하다
be concerned with		...와 관계가 있다
appreciate	동	진가를 알아보다, 인정하다
comparable to		...와 비슷한, ...와 비교할 만한
essentially	부	본질적으로
part	명	부분; (혼합 등의) 비율
whole grain		통 곡물
protein	명	단백질
lower	동	낮추다
blood pressure		혈압
trend	명	유행, 트렌드
keep in shape		건강을 유지하다

dining etiquette		식사 예절
confirm	동	확인해주다
author	동	저술하다, 쓰다
genius	명	천재
passion	명	열정
banquet	명	연회
on the side		부업으로
outstanding	형	뛰어난
boiled	형	삶은
slicer	명	얇게 자르는 기구
garlic	명	마늘
crusher	명	으깨는 도구
grinder	명	가는 도구
similarity	명	유사점
apply	동	신청하다; 쓰다, 적용하다
anchovy	명	멸치

Unit ★ 12 BIOLOGY

infect	동	감염시키다
creature	명	생명체, 생물
crawl	동	기어 다니다
itch	명	간지러움

Reading FORWARD

ADVANCED 1

★ **Word Book** ★

Unit ★ 01 JOBS

bring ... to life	…에 활기를 불어넣다
mission	몡 임무
gallery	몡 미술관, 화랑
curator	몡 큐레이터
task	몡 일
collection	몡 수집품, 소장품
collector	몡 수집가
care for	보살피다, 돌보다
be responsible for	…을 책임지다
organize	동 준비하다, 조직하다
organizational	혱 조직의
exhibition	몡 전시회
theme	몡 주제
borrow	동 빌리다
piece	몡 작품
brief	혱 잠시의; 간단한
description	몡 설명
sculpture	몡 조각품
fascinating	혱 매혹적인; 아주 재미있는
challenging	혱 도전적인
communication	몡 의사소통
purchase	동 구입하다

artwork	명 (특히 박물관의) 미술품
ceramic	명 (*pl.*) 도자기
check out	(도서관에서) 대출받다, 빌리다
register	동 등록하다
librarian	명 사서
install	동 설치하다
suitable	형 적절한
position	명 위치
take back	…을 회수하다
ordinary	형 보통의
valuable	형 소중한; 값비싼
state-of-the-art	형 최첨단의

Unit ★ 02 PLANTS

be made up of	…로 구성되다
individual	형 각각의, 개개의
massive	형 거대한
entire	형 전체의
trunk	명 줄기
root	명 뿌리
secondary	형 이차적인, 부가적인
vertically	부 수직으로

support	⑧ 지탱하다
expand	⑧ 확대하다, 넓히다
branch	⑲ 나뭇가지
shade	⑲ 그늘
merchant	⑲ 상인
legend	⑲ 전설
camp	⑧ 진을 치다, 야영하다
go beyond	…을 넘어서다
shelter	⑲ 쉼터, 보호소
eternal	⑲ 영원한
worship	⑧ 숭배하다
represent	⑧ 나타내다, 상징하다
unity	⑲ 결속, 단결
symbolic	⑲ 상징적인
bark	⑲ 나무껍질
resource	⑲ 자원
unusual	⑲ 특이한
essential	⑲ 필수적인
meaningful	⑲ 의미 있는
outward	⑨ 바깥쪽으로
idealistic	⑲ 이상주의적인
mysterious	⑲ 불가사의한
longevity	⑲ 장수; 수명
status	⑲ 지위
generation	⑲ 세대

coast redwood	세쿼이아(소나뭇과의 나무)
polyphenol	몡 폴리페놀
rot	몡 썩음, 부패
affect	동 영향을 미치다
sticky	혱 끈적끈적한
substance	몡 물질
resistant	혱 저항력 있는, …에 잘 견디는
feature	몡 특징
absorb	동 흡수하다
carbon dioxide	이산화탄소
atmosphere	몡 대기
benefit	몡 혜택, 이득
break out	(안 좋은 일이) 발생하다
survive	동 살아남다
emit	동 내뿜다

Unit ★ 03 ENVIRONMENT

useless	혱 쓸모없는, 소용없는
sawdust	몡 톱밥
reuse	동 재사용하다
eco-friendly	혱 친환경적인
material	몡 재료, 물질

power plant	발전소
opposed	⑱ 반대하는
boil	⑧ 끓이다
steam	⑲ 증기
operate	⑧ 가동하다, 조작하다
generator	⑲ 발전기
methane	⑲ 메탄
decompose	⑧ 분해되다, 부패되다
garbage	⑲ 쓰레기
landfill	⑲ 쓰레기 매립지
consume	⑧ 소비하다
cause	⑧ …을 야기하다, 초래하다 ⑲ 원인
contamination	⑲ 오염
fossil fuel	화석 연료
release	⑧ 풀어주다; 방출하다
cut	⑧ 자르다; 줄이다
obtain	⑧ 얻다, 구하다
dry up	바싹 마르다; 고갈되다
availability	⑲ 유용성
vehicle	⑲ 차량
chemical	⑱ 화학의
industry	⑲ 산업
greenhouse gas	온실가스
efficient	⑱ 효율적인
gallon	⑲ 갤런 (용량의 단위)

Unit ★ 04 ENTERTAINMENT

mushroom	명 버섯
cartoon	명 만화
cartoonist	명 만화가
comic strip	연재만화
made-up	형 지어낸
anniversary	명 기념일
in one's honor	…을 기념하여, 축하하여
mark	동 표시하다; 기념하다
raise	동 (자금을) 모으다
plain	형 평범한; 채색되지 않은
figure	명 숫자; 모형
auction	동 경매로 팔다, 경매에 부치다
feature	동 특별히 포함하다, 특징으로 삼다
charming	형 매력적인
accidentally	부 우연히
inspire	동 영감을 주다
get accustomed to	…에 익숙해지다
fairy	명 요정
folktale	명 민간설화
affection	명 애착
decade	명 10년
term	명 용어, 말

replace	동 대신하다, 대체하다
work out	…을 해결하다, (답 등을) 알아내다
context	명 문맥
intonation	명 억양
confusion	명 혼란
confusing	형 혼란스러운
simplify	동 단순화하다
frequently	부 빈번하게, 자주

Unit ★ 05 HISTORY

merry-go-round	명 회전목마(= carousel)
amusement park	놀이공원
flashing	형 번쩍거리는
catch one's attention	…의 관심을 끌다
innocent	형 무죄인; 순진한, 순수한
ride	명 탈것, 놀이기구
start off	출발하다, 시작하다
on horseback	말을 타고
warrior	명 전사
carve	동 (나무·돌 등에) 새기다[조각하다]
hold up	…을 지탱하다
chain	명 사슬, 쇠줄

pole	똉 기둥
invention	똉 발명; 발명품
evolve	똉 진화하다
evolution	똉 진화
work of art	예술품
detailed	똉 상세한
golden age	황금기, 전성기
Great Depression	대공황
fall out of favor	인기가 떨어지다
fiberglass	똉 유리 섬유
aluminum	똉 알루미늄
weapon	똉 무기
nobleman	똉 귀족
preserve	똉 보호하다; 보존하다
own	똉 소유하다 똉 자기 자신의
regard	똉 …로 여기다
touch	똉 만지기; 느낌, 솜씨
purchase	똉 구입하다
a variety of	다양한
treasure	똉 보물
antique	똉 골동품 똉 골동품인; 고풍스러운
auction	똉 경매
pass down	전해 주다, 물려주다
generation	똉 세대
collectable	똉 수집 가치가 있는 것

Unit ★ 06 SPORTS

extreme	휑 극도의, 극심한
adventure	뗑 모험
challenge	뗑 도전
challenging	휑 도전적인
obvious	휑 명백한; 확실한
Antarctica	뗑 남극대륙
scenery	뗑 경치
encounter	통 접하다, 마주치다
ancient	휑 고대의
monitor	통 감시하다, 관리하다
professional	뗑 전문가
equipment	뗑 장비, 도구
harsh	휑 혹독한
separate	통 (둘 사이를) 가르다
a wide range of	넓은 범위의, 다양한
remarkable	휑 놀랄 만한
participate	통 참가하다
participant	뗑 참가자
limit	뗑 한계
mentally	팀 정신적으로
physically	팀 육체적으로
ultimate	휑 궁극적인

continuous	🕲 지속적인
brief	🕲 짧은
march	🕲 행군
horrible	🕲 끔찍한
trek	🕲 트레킹, 오지 여행
plain	🕲 평원
terrain	🕲 지형, 지역
stunning	🕲 굉장히 멋진
scorching	🕲 몹시 뜨거운
relief	🕲 안도; 경감, 완화
to oneself	혼자 (독차지하는)
sign up for	…에 등록하다
self-reflection	🕲 자아성찰

Unit ★ 07 FESTIVALS

light	🕲 불을 밝히다 🕲 빛
clay	🕲 점토, 찰흙
significant	🕲 중요한
combination	🕲 결합, 조합(물)
row	🕲 열, 줄
assume	🕲 추측하다
harvest	🕲 추수

10

theme	몡 주제
present	휑 존재하는
defeat	몡 패배
prosperous	휑 번영하는
faith	몡 신념; 신앙
decoration	몡 장식
decorate	동 장식하다
feast	동 마음껏 먹다, 잔치에 참여하다
specifically	뷔 명확하게; 구체적으로 말하면
supply	몡 공급; 물자, 용품
exchange	동 교환하다
countless	휑 무수히 많은
explosion	몡 폭발
knit	동 뜨다, 짜다
ornament	몡 장식품
differ	동 다르다
charity	몡 자선
bathe	동 (몸을) 씻다
sacred	휑 신성한
specific	휑 구체적인; 특정한
sin	몡 (종교 · 도덕상의) 죄(악)
forgive	동 용서하다
attract	동 끌어모으다
last	휑 마지막의; 가장 최근의

bride	몡 신부
groom	몡 신랑
best man	신랑 들러리
bridesmaid	몡 신부 들러리
arrange	동 정하다, 준비하다
ceremony	몡 식, 의식
date back to	…까지 거슬러 올라가다
era	몡 시대, 시기
romantic	혱 낭만적인
capture	동 붙잡다
neighboring	혱 이웃의, 근처의
force	동 강요하다
assist	동 돕다
rescue	동 구출하다
ancient	혱 고대의
witness	동 (증인으로서) …에 입회하다 몡 증인
legal	혱 합법적인
function	몡 기능, 역할
be supposed to-v	…하기로 되어 있다
trick	동 속이다
identical	혱 동일한
fool	동 속이다

aggressive	혱 공격적인
hostile	혱 적대적인
mutual	혱 상호간의
maid of honor	(신부 들러리 중 결혼을 하지 않은) 대표 들러리
reception	몡 리셉션, 피로연
toast	몡 건배
newlywed	몡 (pl.) 신혼부부
regardless of	…에 관계없이
accompany	통 동반하다, 동행하다

Unit ★ *09* LITERATURE

alarmed	혱 놀란
tornado	몡 토네이도
yell	통 소리치다
cellar	몡 지하실
pull open	당겨서 열다
spin	통 돌다, 회전하다
rock	통 흔들리다
stormy	혱 폭풍우가 몰아치는
bark	통 짖다
tightly	튀 단단히, 꼭
smash	통 박살내다

resolve	⑧ 해결하다; 결심하다
calmly	⑨ 침착하게
sway	⑧ 흔들리다
howl	⑧ 울부짖다; (바람이) 윙윙거리다
sweep away	…을 쓸어내다, 완전히 없애다
sorrowful	⑩ 슬픈
astonished	⑩ 놀란
somewhere	⑨ 어딘가에
curious	⑩ 호기심 많은
locate	⑧ …에 두다[놓다]
actress	⑪ 여배우
classic	⑪ 고전, 명작

Unit ★ 10 FOOD

yellowish	⑩ 노르스름한
liquid	⑪ 액체 ⑩ 액체의
bubble	⑪ 거품
alcoholic	⑩ 술의, 알코올이 든
beverage	⑪ 음료
barley	⑪ 보리
wheat	⑪ 밀
yeast	⑪ 이스트, 효모균

soaked	형 흠뻑 젖은
chew	동 씹다
flavor	명 풍미, 맛
consumption	명 소비
cinnamon	명 계피
bitter	형 쓴
herb	명 허브, 약초
spice	명 양념, 향신료
refrigerate	동 냉장하다
nausea	명 메스꺼움
priest	명 사제, 성직자
serve	동 제공하다; 근무[복무]하다
class	명 학급; 계층
method	명 방법
currently	부 현재, 지금
variety	명 다양성; 종류
available	형 이용할 수 있는
liquor	명 술
nobleman	명 귀족
state	동 명시하다, 쓰다
hop	명 (pl.) 홉(맥주의 원료)
eventually	부 결국
intent	명 의도
grain	명 곡물
ensure	동 보장하다

reserve	⑧ 남겨두다, 보존하다
promote	⑧ 촉진하다; 홍보하다
superior	⑱ 우수한, 우월한
consistency	⑲ 일관성

Unit★11 PEOPLE

dining etiquette	식사 예절
confirm	⑧ 확인해주다
author	⑧ 저술하다, 쓰다
genius	⑲ 천재
passion	⑲ 열정
banquet	⑲ 연회
on the side	부업으로
outstanding	⑱ 뛰어난
boiled	⑱ 삶은
slicer	⑲ 얇게 자르는 기구
garlic	⑲ 마늘
crusher	⑲ 으깨는 도구
grinder	⑲ 가는 도구
similarity	⑲ 유사점
apply	⑧ 신청하다; 쓰다, 적용하다
anchovy	⑲ 멸치

innovative	혱 혁신적인
recognize	동 알아보다; 인정하다
multi-talented	혱 다재다능한
enthusiasm	몡 열정, 열의
behave	동 행동하다; 예의 바르게 행동하다
be concerned with	…와 관계가 있다
appreciate	동 진가를 알아보다, 인정하다
comparable to	…와 비슷한, …와 비교할 만한
essentially	閈 본질적으로
part	몡 부분; (혼합 등의) 비율
whole grain	통 곡물
protein	몡 단백질
lower	동 낮추다
blood pressure	혈압
trend	몡 유행, 트렌드
keep in shape	건강을 유지하다

Unit ★ 12 BIOLOGY

infect	동 감염시키다
creature	몡 생명체, 생물
crawl	동 기어 다니다
itch	몡 간지러움

section	몡 부분
fill in	채우다
scratch	통 긁다
repetitive	혱 반복적인
lyric	몡 (pl.) 가사
commercial	몡 광고
ringtone	몡 벨 소리, 신호음
perfectly	뮈 완전히, 지극히
symptom	몡 징후, 증상
get stuck	꼼짝 못하게 되다
frequently	뮈 자주, 빈번히
criticize	통 비판하다, 비평하다
analyze	통 분석하다
phenomenon	몡 현상
idle	통 하는 일 없이 지내다
seashell	몡 조개껍데기
roar	몡 (바람·바다 등이) 울부짖는 듯한 소리 통 (바람·파도 등이) 굉음을 내다
have to do with	…와 관련이 있다
hollow	혱 (속이) 빈

Unit ★ 13 ANIMALS

vision	몡 시력
rely on	…에 의지하다
extremely	틧 극히, 극단적으로
distinguish	통 구별하다, 식별하다
tell	통 말하다; 구별하다
shade	몡 그늘; 색조
forward	틧 앞으로
depth perception	거리[깊이] 감각
when it comes to	…에 관해서
surroundings	몡 (pl.) 주변, 환경
directly	틧 바로
surface	몡 표면
fair	혱 공정한; 타당한
accurate	혱 정확한
discriminate	통 식별하다, 분간하다
based on	…에 근거하여
solely	틧 오직
appearance	몡 외모, 모습
motionless	혱 움직임이 없는
gesture	몡 제스처, 몸짓
in addition to	… 외에도
posture	몡 자세

keep in mind	명심하다
train	⑧ 훈련하다
command	⑲ 명령
dull	⑲ 지루한; 둔한

Unit ★ 14 HEALTH

hug	⑲ 포옹 ⑧ 포옹하다
sensation	⑲ 느낌; 선풍, 돌풍
clip	⑲ 핀, 클립; (영화 등의) 클립(일부만 따로 떼어서 보여 주는 부분)
stand out	두드러지다
impact	⑲ 영향
pleasurable	⑲ 즐거운
chemical	⑲ 화학 물질
dopamine	⑲ 도파민
oxytocin	⑲ 옥시토신
activate	⑧ 작동시키다, 활성화시키다
be concerned with	…와 관계가 있다
lead to	(결과적으로) …에 이르다, …하게 되다
save	⑧ 남겨두다
be willing to-v	기꺼이 …하다
workmate	⑲ (직장) 동료

20

mental	혱 정신적인
be associated with	…와 연관이 있다
caring	몡 상냥함, 친절함
bonding	몡 유대
thanks to	…의 덕택으로
arrival	몡 도착
notice	동 알아차리다
cardboard	몡 판지
sign	몡 표지판
get down	…을 굽히다, 구부리다
part	동 헤어지다; 갈라지다
comfort	동 위로하다
respond to	…에 응하다

Unit ★ 15 FASHION

keep current with	…의 동향을 알다
full figured	(여성이) 체격이 큰; (옷 등이) 큰 사이즈의
decade	몡 10년
realistic	혱 현실적인
skinny	혱 깡마른
die from	…로 죽다
eating disorder	식이 장애

aim for	…을 목표로 하다
responsibility	명 책임감
former	형 이전의
plus-size	형 체격이 큰, 큰 사이즈의
colleague	명 동료
be tired of	…가 지겹다
overlook	동 간과하다
intention	명 의도
draw attention to	…에 관심을 끌어들이다
hazard	명 위험
at risk	위험에 처한
representative	명 대표자
with time	시간이 흐름에 따라
trendy	형 최신 유행의
disregard	동 무시하다
unavoidable	형 불가피한
outfit	명 옷
promote	동 장려하다, 촉진하다
ideal	명 이상형 형 이상적인
regulate	동 규제하다
due to	…때문에
starvation	명 기아
ban	동 금지하다 명 금지(법)
runway	명 패션쇼 무대
boycott	동 불매 운동하다

| expel | 동 내쫓다, 쫓아버리다 |
| take action | 동 조치를 취하다 |

Unit★16 PSYCHOLOGY

donation	명 기부, 기증
charity	명 자선 단체; 자선
originate	동 유래하다
conduct	동 수행하다
nun	명 수녀
measure	동 측정하다, 재다
immunoglobulin	명 면역 글로불린 항체
defense	명 방어; 방어물
significantly	부 상당히, 크게
volunteer	명 자원봉사자 동 자원봉사를 하다
helper's high	다른 이를 도울 때 느끼는 만족감
calm	명 고요, 평온
chronic	형 만성적인
insomnia	명 불면증
evidence	명 증거
give it a try	시도하다, 한번 해보다
dedicate	동 헌신하다
immune system	면역 체계

worsen	⑧ 악화시키다
religious order	수도회
welfare	⑲ 복지, 행복
missionary	⑲ 선교사
orphan	⑧ 고아로 만들다
branch	⑲ 나뭇가지; 지사
relief	⑲ 안도; 구호, 구호물자
disaster	⑲ 재난, 재해
alcoholic	⑲ 알코올 중독자
homeless	⑱ 집이 없는
sufferer	⑲ 고통받는 사람, 환자
establish	⑧ 설립하다

Unit ★ *17* SPACE

gaze	⑧ 바라보다, 응시하다
moon	⑲ 달; 위성
shape	⑧ (중요한 영향을 미쳐) 형성하다
mythology	⑲ 신화
habitable	⑱ 살 수 있는, 거주할 만한
obviously	⑭ 분명히
lunar	⑱ 달의
solar	⑱ 태양의

eclipse	명 (일식·월식의) 식
rotation	명 회전, 자전
rotate	동 회전하다
billion	명 10억
stretch	동 퍼지다, 뻗어 나가다
banded	형 줄무늬 모양의, 띠의
constantly	부 지속적으로
howling	형 휘몰아치는
exchange	명 교환
probable	형 (어떤 일이) 있음 직한
windstorm	명 폭풍
enormous	형 거대한
enhance	동 향상시키다
restrict	동 제한하다
accelerate	동 가속화하다
continuous	형 지속적인
presence	명 존재
paw	명 (동물의) 발
rebirth	명 부활
plenty of	많은
superstition	명 미신
medieval	형 중세의
lunatic	명 미치광이 형 미친
transform	동 변신하다
werewolf	명 늑대 인간

occupy	⑧ 점유하다, 차지하다
central	⑧ 중심의
background	⑲ 배경
along with	…와 함께
regardless of	…와 무관하게
according to	…에 의하면

Unit★18 MYSTERIES

historian	⑲ 사학자
map	⑲ 지도 ⑧ 지도를 만들다[그리다]
admiral	⑲ 해군 장성, 제독
inaccurate	⑧ 부정확한
accurate	⑧ 정확한
accurately	⑨ 정확하게
accuracy	⑲ 정확도
circular	⑧ 원형의, 둥근
transfer	⑧ 옮기다, 이동하다
grid	⑲ 격자무늬; (지도의) 격자 눈금
globe	⑲ 지구본
correct	⑧ 바로잡다, 정정하다
Antarctica	⑲ 남극대륙
antarctic	⑧ 남극의

coastline	몡 해안선
consult	통 상담하다; 참고하다
civilization	몡 문명
as to	…에 관해서는
alien	몡 외계인
outer space	우주 공간
existence	몡 존재
navy	몡 해군
empire	몡 제국
navigation	몡 항해(술)
technique	몡 기법, 기술
compass	몡 나침반
direction	몡 방향
contribution	몡 기부금; 기여, 이바지
execute	통 처형하다
refuse	통 거절[거부]하다
unjust	혱 불공평한, 부당한
biography	몡 전기, 일대기
achievement	몡 업적

Unit ★ 19 ART

Impressionist	몡 인상파 화가

intensity	몡 강도; 명암
tone	몡 어조; 색조
escape	동 탈출하다; 눈에 띄지 않다
abstract	혱 추상적인
vibrant	혱 강렬한, 선명한
theory	몡 이론
recreate	동 재현하다
blurry	혱 흐릿한
dull	혱 따분한; 칙칙한
compensate	동 보상하다; 보완하다
convinced	혱 확신하는
surgery	몡 수술
intentional	혱 의도적인
intend	동 의도하다
hypothesis	몡 가설 (*pl.* hypotheses)
attempt	동 시도하다
overcome	동 극복하다
hardship	몡 고난
have difficulty v-ing	…하는 데 어려움을 겪다
confess	동 고백하다
treatment	몡 치료
Impressionism	몡 인상주의
surface	몡 표면
energetic	혱 활기가 넘치는
emphasize	동 강조하다

28

capture	동 (필름 · 화폭 등에) 담다
fleeting	형 순식간의, 잠깐 동안의
joyous	형 기쁨을 주는
last	동 지속되다

Unit ★ 20 MEDICINE

get a shot	주사를 맞다
replace	동 대체하다
pill	명 알약
microchip	명 마이크로 칩
place	동 놓다
seal	동 밀봉하다
break down	분해되다
save	동 구하다; …하지 않아도 되게 하다
melt away	녹아 사라지다
needle	명 바늘
undergo	동 겪다, 받다
operation	명 수술
get over	회복하다, 극복하다
forward	부 앞으로, 앞쪽에
spit out	뱉다
throat	명 목

swallow	동 삼키다
alternatively	부 그 대신에, 그렇지 않으면
crush	동 가루로 만들다
strategy	명 전략, 방법
offootivc	형 효과가 있는
proper	형 적합한
medicate	동 약을 투여하다

Reading
FORWARD

ADVANCED 1

★ Answer Key ★

Reading FORWARD

ADVANCED 1

★ Answer Key ★

★Art Gallery Curators

1 b   **2** d   **3** They can discover the fascinating stories behind the art.   **4** d   **5** b   **6** *1)* T *2)* F

예술작품에 생기를 불어넣는 것, 그것이 미술관 큐레이터로서의 제 임무입니다. 안녕하세요! 저는 Vivien이에요. 제가 여러분에게 제 직업에 대해 말씀드릴게요.

미술관 큐레이터는 많은 다양한 일들을 합니다. 제 가장 중요한 일 중 하나는 미술 소장품들을 돌보는 것입니다. 저는 모든 것이 어디에 있는지를 알아야 하고, 모든 예술품이 제대로 관리되고 있는지 확인해야 합니다. 저는 또한 전시회를 준비하는 일도 책임지고 있습니다. 일 년에 네 번에서 다섯 번, 우리 미술관은 특별 전시회를 엽니다. 전시회를 준비할 때 저는 그것을 위한 주제를 선정하고, 무엇을 보여줄지를 고릅니다. 저는 전시회를 위한 예술작품들을 대여하기 위해 예술가와 다른 박물관, 그리고 개인 수집가들과 이야기를 합니다. (어떤 예술가들은 그들 작품의 특별 전시회를 통해 유명해집니다.) 때때로 저는 미술관을 위해 새로운 예술품을 구입하기도 합니다. 저는 지금 그리고 미래에도 사람들이 감상하는 데 관심 있어 할 작품들을 골라야 합니다.

하지만 제가 제 직업에서 가장 좋아하는 것은 사람들이 예술에 대해 알도록 돕는 것입니다. 저는 모든 그림과 조각품 옆 벽에 붙일 라벨과 간단한 설명을 작성합니다. 그것들을 읽으면, 사람들은 그 예술작품 뒤에 있는 흥미로운 이야기들을 알 수 있습니다. 저는 제가 사람들이 놀라운 예술의 세계에 눈을 뜨도록 돕는다고 생각하고 싶습니다.

저는 미술관 큐레이터인 것이 좋습니다. 그 직업은 정말로 창조적이고 도전적입니다. 또한, 그것은 저를 제가 가장 좋아하는 것인 예술에 가까이 가도록 해줍니다. 여러분이 예술을 좋아하고, 훌륭한 의사소통 능력과 조직 능력이 있다면, 미술관 큐레이터는 여러분에게 완벽한 직업이 될 수 있습니다!

어휘   bring … to life …에 활기를 불어넣다   mission[míʃən] 명 임무   gallery[gǽləri] 명 미술관, 화랑 curator[kjuəréitər] 명 큐레이터   task[tæsk] 명 일   collection[kəlékʃən] 명 수집품, 소장품 (collector 명 수집가)   care for 보살피다, 돌보다   be responsible for …을 책임지다 organize[ɔ́ːrgənàiz] 동 준비하다, 조직하다 (organizational 형 조직의)   exhibition[èksəbíʃən] 명 전시회   theme[θiːm] 명 주제   borrow[bɑ́rou] 동 빌리다   piece[piːs] 명 작품   brief[briːf] 형 잠시의; *간단한   description[diskrípʃən] 명 설명   sculpture[skʌ́lptʃər] 명 조각품 fascinating[fǽsənèitiŋ] 형 매혹적인; *아주 재미있는   challenging[tʃǽlindʒiŋ] 형 도전적인 communication[kəmjùːnəkéiʃən] 명 의사소통   [문제] purchase[pə́ːrtʃəs] 동 구입하다 artwork[ɑ́ːrtwə̀ːrk] 명 (특히 박물관의) 미술품

구문   4행   I have to know [**where** everything is] and ….
　　　　　• where 이하는 '의문사 + 주어 + 동사' 어순의 간접의문문으로, 동사 know의 목적어 역할을 함

　　　7행   [**When preparing** for an exhibition], I choose a theme for it and select *what to show*.
　　　　　• When preparing 이하는 때를 나타내는 분사구문으로, 의미를 명확하게 하기 위해 접속사를 생략하지 않음
　　　　　• what to-v: '무엇을 …할지'의 의미로, 동사 select의 목적어 역할을 함

　　　11행   I have to choose items [**that** people will be interested in …].
　　　　　• that 이하는 items를 수식하는 목적격 관계대명사절

　　　13행   The thing [(that) **I love** most about my job], though, is *helping* people *learn* about art.
　　　　　• I love 앞에 The thing을 선행사로 하는 목적격 관계대명사가 생략되어 있음
　　　　　• help + 목적어 + 동사원형: …가 ~하도록 돕다

　　　19행   It also **lets** me **get** close to my favorite thing: art.

• 사역동사(let) + 목적어 + 동사원형: ···가 ~하게 하다

STRATEGIC ORGANIZER   collection, Organizes, Buys, find out

EXPANDING KNOWLEDGE

1 c   **2** d

당신은 예술품 도서관이 있다는 것을 알고 있었는가? 그것은 Art Lending Library인데, 여기에서 당신은 예술가의 소장품들을 무료로 빌릴 수 있다. 도자기, 소형 조각상, 그림, 소묘, 사진 등을 포함하여 선택의 폭이 광범위하다. 그러나 예술품을 빌리기 전에 당신은 도서관에 등록해야 한다. 그러고 나서, 당신이 원하는 예술품을 고르면 사서가 그 작품을 당신의 집으로 가지고 와서, 그것을 적절한 장소에 설치해준다. 오직 사서만이 그것을 만지도록 허용된다. 3개월 후에, 사서가 그것을 도서관으로 회수하기 위해 다시 온다. 이 서비스를 통해, Art Lending Library는 보통 사람들이 예술의 아름다움과 즐거움을 그들의 가정으로 가져가도록 돕는다.

어휘   ceramic[sərǽmik] 몡 (pl.) 도자기   check out (도서관에서) 대출받다, 빌리다   register[rédʒistər] 동 등록하다   librarian[laibrɛ́əriən] 몡 사서   install[instɔ́:l] 동 설치하다   suitable[súːtəbl] 휑 적절한   position[pəzíʃən] 몡 위치   take back ···을 회수하다   ordinary[ɔ́ːrdənèri] 휑 보통의 [문제] valuable[vǽljuəbl] 소중한; *값비싼   state-of-the-art[stéitəvðiáːrt] 휑 최첨단의

구문   1행   It is the Art Lending Library, **where** you can borrow works from ....
 • where는 the Art Lending Library를 보충 설명하는 계속적 용법의 관계부사
9행   After three months, the librarian comes again **to _take_ it back** to the library.
 • to take: '···하기 위해'라는 의미로, 목적을 나타내는 부사적 용법의 to부정사
 • take it back: '동사 + 부사'로 이루어진 동사구의 목적어로 대명사가 올 때, 목적어는 반드시 동사와 부사 사이에 위치함

VOCABULARY REVIEW

A   **1** task   **2** collection   **3** gallery   **4** label
B   **1** register   **2** exhibition   **3** creative   **4** borrow   **5** installed   **C**   **1** b   **2** d

unit
02 PLANTS

pp. 12-15

Banyan Tree

1 d   **2** b   **3** Because Indian merchants used to meet under banyans to discuss business.   **4** b
5 c   **6** 1) T 2) F

숲은 보통 많은 개개의 나무들로 구성된다. 그러나 어떤 경우에는, 단 하나의 나무가 전체 숲만큼 거대하게 보일 수 있다. 인도의 바니안나무는 여러 개의 다른 나무들처럼 보이는 방식으로 자란다.

대부분의 다른 나무들처럼, 바니안나무는 하나의 줄기로 시작된다. 하지만 시간이 지나면서 그 나무는 땅의 표면을 따라 바깥으로 뿌리를 뻗는다. 이 뿌리들은 수직으로 자라는 이차 줄기를 만들어서 나무에서 퍼져 나가는 나뭇가지를 지탱하도록 도와준다. 이 과정은 나무의 일생 동안 계속되어, 가장 오래된 바니안나무는 너비가 200미터에 이르는 면적을 뒤덮을 수 있다.

그 거대한 크기 덕에, 바니안나무는 사람들이 그늘에서 쉬기 위해 모여드는 만남의 장소로 이용되어 왔다. 사실, 그 나무의 이름은 'bania', 즉 상인이라는 단어에서 유래한 것인데, 왜냐하면 인도의 상인들은 사업을 의논하러 바니안나무 아래에 모이곤 했기 때문이다. 심지어 알렉산더 대왕의 7,000명의 군대가 한때 단 한 그루의 바니안나무 아래에서 진을 쳤다는 전설도 있다.

그러나 인도 문화에서 바니안나무의 중요성은 쉼터 이상이다. 그것은 영생의 상징으로 여겨지며 인도인들에게 흔히 숭배를 받는다. 바니안나무는 또한 인도의 국가적 상징이다. 그것의 연결된 뿌리, 줄기와 가지는 인도의 단결을 의미한다. 상징적 중요성 이상으로, 그 나무는 또한 <u>실용적인</u> 재료의 원천이기도 하다. 그것의 목재와 껍질은 종이로 만들어지고, 뿌리는 밧줄과 피부용 크림으로 만들어지며, 씨는 약재로 사용된다. 바니안나무가 왜 그렇게 긴 시간 동안 사람들의 삶과 이야기의 일부가 되었는지를 이해하기는 쉽다.

어휘 be made up of …로 구성되다   individual[ìndəvídʒuəl] 혱 각각의, 개개의   massive[mǽsiv] 혱 거대한   entire[intáiər] 혱 전체의   trunk[trʌŋk] 몡 줄기   root[ruːt] 몡 뿌리   secondary[sékəndèri] 혱 이차적인, 부가적인   vertically[və́ːrtikəli] 閏 수직으로   support[səpɔ́ːrt] 동 지탱하다   expand[ikspǽnd] 동 확대하다, 넓히다   branch[brǽntʃ] 몡 나뭇가지   shade[ʃeid] 몡 그늘   merchant[mə́ːrtʃənt] 몡 상인   legend[lédʒənd] 몡 전설   camp[kæmp] 동 진을 치다, 야영하다   go beyond …을 넘어서다   shelter[ʃéltər] 몡 쉼터, 보호소   eternal[itə́ːrnəl] 혱 영원한   worship[wə́ːrʃip] 동 숭배하다   represent[rèprizént] 동 나타내다, 상징하다   unity[júːnəti] 몡 결속, 단결   symbolic[simbálik] 혱 상징적인   bark[baːrk] 몡 나무껍질   [문제] resource[ríːsɔːrs] 몡 자원   unusual[ʌnjúːʒuəl] 혱 특이한   essential[isénʃəl] 혱 필수적인   meaningful[míːniŋfəl] 혱 의미 있는   outward[áutwərd] 閏 바깥쪽으로   idealistic[aidìəlístik] 혱 이상주의적인   mysterious[mistíəriəs] 혱 불가사의한   longevity[landʒévəti] 몡 장수; *수명   status[stéitəs] 몡 지위   generation[dʒènəréiʃən] 몡 세대

구문 2행 But in some cases, a single tree can appear **as massive as** an entire forest.
　　　• as + 형용사의 원급 + as: …만큼 ～한
　　9행 These roots create secondary trunks [**that** grow vertically and *help support* …].
　　　• that 이하는 secondary trunks를 수식하는 주격 관계대명사절
　　　• help + 동사원형: …하도록 돕다
　　17행 …, banyans have been used as meeting places [**where** people gather …].
　　　• where 이하는 meeting places를 수식하는 관계부사절
　　28행 It's easy [**to see** *why the banyan tree has been a part of* …].
　　　• It은 가주어이고, to see 이하가 진주어
　　　• why 이하는 '의문사 + 주어 + 동사' 어순의 간접의문문으로, 동사 see의 목적어 역할을 함

STRATEGIC SUMMARY spreading, social, symbol, useful

EXPANDING KNOWLEDGE

1 a **2** 1) T 2) F

세쿼이아는 세상의 모든 다른 나무들보다 높이 서 있다. 발견된 것 중 가장 키가 큰 세쿼이아는 높이가 379.1피트로, 그것은 런던에 있는 빅벤 탑보다 더 높다. 세쿼이아는 또한 오래 사는 것으로도 유명하다. 어떤 세쿼이아는 2,000년 또는 그보다 더 오래 산다. 그 나무가 그렇게 오래 살 수 있는 것은 폴리페놀이 많아서, 벌레나 부패가 나무에 영향을 주지 않기 때문이다. 게다가, 나무껍질에는 끈적끈적한 물질이 많아서 불에 저항력이 강하다. 세쿼이아의 또 다른 큰 특징은 잎에서부터 뿌리로 수분을 내려보낼 수 있다는 것이다. 이는 그 나무들이 잎으로 안개를 바로 흡수하기 때문에 가능하다. 마지막으로, 세쿼이아 숲은 다른 어떤 숲보다 대기로부터 이산화탄소를 더 잘 제거하기 때문에 지구에 아주 좋다.

어휘 coast redwood 세쿼이아(소나뭇과의 나무)   polyphenol[pàlifíːnoul] 몡 폴리페놀   rot[rat] 몡 썩음, 부패   affect[əfékt] 동 영향을 미치다   sticky[stíki] 혱 끈적끈적한   substance[sʌ́bstəns] 몡 물질   resistant[rizístənt] 혱 저항력 있는, …에 잘 견디는   feature[fíːtʃər] 몡 특징   absorb[æbsɔ́ːrb] 동 흡수하다   carbon dioxide 이산화탄소   atmosphere[ǽtməsfìər] 몡 대기   [문제] benefit[bénəfit] 몡 혜택, 이득   break out (안 좋은 일이) 발생하다   survive[sərváiv]

동 살아남다　emit[imít] 동 내뿜다

구문　12행 ... carbon dioxide from the atmosphere **better than any other forest**.
　　　　• 비교급 + than any other + 단수명사: '어떤 …보다 더 ~한'의 의미로, 최상급을 나타냄

VOCABULARY REVIEW
A **1** represent **2** bark **3** eternal **4** merchant
B **1** substance **2** entire **3** longevity **4** resistant **5** outward　　**C** **1** d **2** a

unit
03 ENVIRONMENT pp. 16-19

Biomass Energy
1 c **2** b **3** c **4** Because it releases less carbon dioxide than fossil fuels. **5** d **6** c

일반적으로 우리는 쓰레기가 쓸모없다고 생각하고 그것을 쉽게 버린다. 하지만 나뭇가지, 톱밥, 그리고 동물의 배설물과 같은 일부 쓰레기는 바이오매스를 포함하고 있는데, 이것은 바이오매스 에너지라고 알려진 친환경 에너지를 생산하는 데 재사용될 수 있다.

그러면 어떻게 우리는 아무도 원하지 않는 것처럼 보이는 물질로부터 에너지를 얻을 수 있을까? 한 가지 방법은 발전소에서 쓰레기를 태우는 것이다. (어떤 사람들은 안전상의 우려 때문에 주택 근처에 발전소를 세우는 것에 반대한다.) 쓰레기를 태워서 생기는 열은 물을 끓이는 데 사용되는데, 이것은 증기를 만들어낸다. 그리고 나서, 증기의 에너지는 발전기를 작동시켜서 전기를 만든다. 또 다른 방법은 쓰레기 매립지에서 부패하는 쓰레기나 소, 돼지와 닭의 배설물에서 생겨나는 메탄가스를 사용하는 것이다. 이 가스는 모이면 에너지를 만들어내기 위해 태워진다.

바이오매스 에너지를 생산하고 소비하는 것은 여러 면에서 도움이 된다. 첫째로, 우리는 쓰레기의 일부를 태움으로써 그 양을 줄일 수 있다. 그러지 않으면, 그 쓰레기는 결국 쓰레기 매립지로 보내져 아마도 오염을 일으킬 것이다. 게다가, 바이오매스를 이용하는 것은 석유, 석탄, 그리고 천연가스와 같은 화석 연료의 사용을 줄일 수 있다. 바이오매스는 화석 연료보다 이산화탄소를 덜 배출하기 때문에 환경친화적이기까지 하다. 뿐만 아니라, 그것은 온실 효과의 주요 원인 중 하나인 메탄가스를 줄여준다.

요즈음, 에너지 자원을 얻기가 점점 더 어렵고 더 비싸지고 있다. 그러니 대신 바이오매스를 사용해 보는 것은 어떨까? 그것은 경제적이고, 지구 상에 식물과 동물이 사는 한 절대 고갈되지 않을 것이다.

어휘　useless[júːslis] 형 쓸모없는, 소용없는　sawdust[sɔ́ːdʌ̀st] 명 톱밥　reuse[riːjúːz] 동 재사용하다
eco-friendly[ékoufréndli] 형 친환경적인　material[mətíəriəl] 명 재료, 물질　power plant 발전소
opposed[əpóuzd] 형 반대하는　boil[bɔil] 동 끓이다　steam[stiːm] 명 증기　operate[ápərèit]
동 가동하다, 조작하다　generator[dʒénərèitər] 명 발전기　methane[méθein] 명 메탄
decompose[dìːkəmpóuz] 동 분해되다, 부패하다　garbage[gáːrbidʒ] 명 쓰레기　landfill[lǽndfìl]
명 쓰레기 매립지　consume[kənsúːm] 동 소비하다　cause[kɔːz] 동 …을 야기하다, 초래하다 명 원인
contamination[kəntæ̀mənéiʃən] 명 오염　fossil fuel 화석 연료　release[rilíːs] 동 풀어주다;
*방출하다　cut[kʌt] 동 자르다; *줄이다　obtain[əbtéin] 동 얻다, 구하다　dry up 바싹 마르다;
*고갈되다　[문제] availability[əvèiləbíləti] 명 유용성

구문　3행 ... contains biomass, **which** can be reused to produce eco-friendly energy [*known*
　　　　as biomass energy].
　　　　• which: biomass를 보충 설명하는 계속적 용법의 주격 관계대명사
　　　　• known 이하는 eco-friendly energy를 수식하는 과거분사구
6행 So how can we get energy from material [**that** nobody seems to want]?

- that 이하는 material을 수식하는 목적격 관계대명사절

25행 These days, **it** is getting harder and more expensive [**to obtain** energy resources].
- it은 가주어이고, to obtain 이하가 진주어

26행 It is economical, and it will never dry up **as long as** plants and animals *live* on Earth.
- as long as: …하는 한
- live: 조건을 나타내는 부사절에서는 현재시제가 미래시제를 대신함

STRATEGIC SUMMARY burning, garbage, fossil fuels, cheap

EXPANDING KNOWLEDGE

1 c **2** *1)* F *2)* T

옥수수에서 연료의 한 종류를 얻을 수 있다는 것을 알고 있었는가? 그것은 옥수수 에탄올인데, 이는 옥수수에 있는 당을 알코올로 변화시켜 생산될 수 있다. 옥수수 에탄올은 몇몇 종류의 엔진에 사용하기 좋은 연료이다. 그것은 또한 차량을 운행하는 데 사용되며 화학 산업에서 매우 유용하다. 게다가, 옥수수 에탄올은 환경친화적인 것으로 여겨지는데, 왜냐하면 그것은 화석 연료보다 더 적은 양의 온실가스를 배출하기 때문이다. 하지만 그것은 효율적인 연료는 아니다. 25갤런의 에탄올을 생산하기 위해서는, 450파운드의 옥수수가 필요하다. 그것은 한 사람이 1년 동안 먹을 수 있을 만큼 많다! 그러므로 우리가 더 많은 옥수수 에탄올을 사용할수록, 우리는 훨씬 더 많은 옥수수가 필요하게 된다. 그 결과, 옥수수 가격이 오르고, 이는 옥수수를 사용하여 생산되는 모든 것에 영향을 미친다.

어휘 vehicle[ví:ikl] 몡 차량 chemical[kémikəl] 휑 화학의 industry[índəstri] 몡 산업
greenhouse gas 온실가스 efficient[ifíʃənt] 휑 효율적인 gallon[gǽlən] 몡 갤런 (용량의 단위)

구문 1행 It's corn ethanol, **which** can be produced by changing ….
- which: corn ethanol을 보충 설명하는 계속적 용법의 주격 관계대명사

8행 That's **as much as** a person could eat in a year!
- as + 형용사의 원급 + as: …만큼 ~한

9행 As a result, the price of corn rises, **which** affects everything [*that* is produced using corn].
- which: 앞의 절을 선행사로 하는 계속적 용법의 주격 관계대명사
- that 이하는 everything을 수식하는 주격 관계대명사절

VOCABULARY REVIEW

A **1** release **2** operate **3** decompose **4** landfill
B **1** steam **2** reusing **3** industry **4** opposed **5** efficient   C **1** b **2** a

★unit★
04 ENTERTAINMENT pp. 20-23

★ *The Smurfs*

1 c **2** d **3** It sent the Smurfs on a one-year worldwide tour to raise money. **4** b **5** b **6** d

*Les Schtroumpfs*를 아는가? 그들은 체구가 작고 파랗고, 하얀 모자를 쓰며, 숲 속 깊이 숨겨진 버섯 모양의 집에 산다. 이 인기 있는 만화 캐릭터들은 1958년 벨기에 만화가 Peyo에 의해 창조되었다. 그들은 영어로는 스머프라고 알려져 있다.

원래 그들은 다른 연재만화인 *구멍이 여섯 개인 피리*의 보조 캐릭터였다. 그 이야기가 출간된 후, 스머프는 매우 인기 있어서 그들만의 연재만화가 주어졌다. 그들의 이름과 관련하여 또 다른 재미있는 사실이 있다. 어느 날 Peyo는 친구와 함께 식사하다가 '소금'이라는 단어를 갑자기 잊어버렸다. 그는 대신 schtroumpf를 달라고 했고, 이 지어낸 단어가 곧 그와 친구 사이의 농담이 되었다. 결국, Schtroumpfs는 그 캐릭터의 이름이 되었다.

시간이 지나면서, 스머프는 세계적으로 인기를 얻었다. 2008년에는 그들의 50주년이 기념되었다. 그들을 기념하여 벨기에는 그들의 모습이 찍힌 특별한 5유로 동전을 제작했다. 유니세프도 모금을 위한 1년간의 세계 여행에 스머프들을 보내어 기념일을 축하했다. 채색되지 않은 스머프 모형들이 유명 인사들에 의해 색칠된 다음 경매에 부쳐졌고, 유니세프의 교육 프로그램을 위해 십만 유로 넘게 벌어들였다.

오래되었지만, 스머프는 해마다 계속 성공적이다. 그들이 나오는 대중가요와 비디오, 컴퓨터 게임은 전 세계적으로 잘 팔린다. 스머프 텔레비전 쇼, 스머프 영화, 스머프 테마파크, 심지어 스머프가 나오는 연극도 있다! 사람들은 Peyo의 매력적인 파란 만화 캐릭터들을 절대 지겨워하지 않을 것처럼 보인다.

어휘 mushroom[mʌ́ʃruːm] 명 버섯 cartoon[kɑːrtúːn] 명 만화 (cartoonist 명 만화가) comic strip 연재만화 made-up[méidʌp] 형 지어낸 anniversary[æ̀nəvə́ːrsəri] 명 기념일 in one's honor …을 기념하여, 축하하여 mark[mɑːrk] 동 표시하다; *기념하다 raise[reiz] 동 (자금을) 모으다 plain[plein] 형 평범한; *채색되지 않은 figure[fíɡjər] 명 숫자; *모형 auction[ɔ́ːkʃən] 동 경매로 팔다, 경매에 부치다 feature[fíːtʃər] 동 특별히 포함하다, 특징으로 삼다 charming[tʃɑ́ːrmiŋ] 형 매력적인 [문제] accidentally[æ̀ksədéntəli] 부 우연히 inspire[inspáiər] 동 영감을 주다 get accustomed to …에 익숙해지다 fairy[fέəri] 명 요정 folktale[fóuktèil] 명 민간설화 affection[əfékʃən] 명 애착

구문 2행 …, and they live in mushroom-shaped houses [**hidden** deep in the forest].
     • hidden 이하는 mushroom-shaped houses를 수식하는 과거분사구

  8행 One day, Peyo suddenly forgot the word for "salt" [**while eating** with a friend].
     • while eating 이하는 때를 나타내는 분사구문으로, 의미를 명확하게 하기 위해 접속사를 생략하지 않음

  16행 … and then auctioned off, [**earning** more than 100,000 euros …].
     • earning 이하는 연속동작을 나타내는 분사구문(= and it earned)

STRATEGIC ORGANIZER popular, strip, mistake, tour, featured

EXPANDING KNOWLEDGE

1 a **2** *1)* T *2)* F

벨기에의 만화 영화 시리즈인 *스머프*는 오십 년 넘게 국제적인 성공작이었다. 그런데 원래 스머프에게 그들만의 언어가 있었다는 것을 알았는가? 그들 언어의 주요 특징 중 하나는 '스머프'라는 용어가 종종 다른 단어를 대신했다는 것이다. 예를 들어, 한 캐릭터가 "나는 오늘 숲에 갈 거야."라고 말하려고 했을 때, 그 표현은 '오늘 나는 스머프에 스머프할 거야.'가 되었다. '스머프'라는 단어가 의미하는 것은 문맥과 억양을 통해 파악해야 했다. 그러나 이것은 때때로 그 프로를 보는 사람들에게 큰 혼란을 일으켰다. 그래서 덜 혼란스럽게 만들기 위해 언어는 단순화되어야 했다. 그러나 '스머프'라는 단어는 오늘날의 시리즈에서도 여전히 자주 사용된다.

어휘 decade[dékeid] 명 10년 term[təːrm] 명 용어, 말 replace[ripléis] 동 대신하다, 대체하다 work out …을 해결하다, (답 등을) 알아내다 context[kántekst] 명 문맥 intonation[ìntounéiʃən] 명 억양 confusion[kənfjúːʒən] 명 혼란 (confusing 형 혼란스러운) simplify[símpləfài] 동 단순화하다 frequently[fríːkwəntli] 부 빈번하게, 자주

구문 1행 The Belgian animated series *The Smurfs* **has been** an international hit ….
     • has been: '…해 왔다'의 의미로, 계속을 나타내는 현재완료

  6행 **What** the word "smurf" meant had to be worked out from the context ….

• what: '…하는 것'의 의미로, 선행사를 포함하는 관계대명사

VOCABULARY REVIEW
A **1** decade **2** replace **3** secondary **4** feature
B **1** published **2** characteristic **3** confusing **4** simplify **5** originally **C** **1** b **2** a

★unit★ 05 HISTORY

pp. 24-27

★Carousels

1 d **2** b **3** It was used to show one's horse riding skills. **4** a **5** a **6** 1) F 2) T

사람들이 놀이공원에 있는 회전목마 앞에 서 있다. 번쩍거리는 불빛, 화려한 색깔, 그리고 시끄러운 서커스 음악이 모두 그들의 관심을 끈다. 그들은 색이 칠해진 말 중 한 마리에 올라타 계속 돌고 싶어 한다. 그처럼 순수한 아이들의 놀이기구가 전쟁을 위한 훈련 도구로 시작되었다는 것은 믿기 어렵다.

12세기에 터키 병사들은 전투를 준비하기 위해 말을 타고 경기를 했다. 그 경기를 본 스페인 전사들이 그것을 carosella라고 명명했는데, 이는 '작은 전쟁'을 의미한다. 그들은 그 경기를 유럽에 들여왔고, 결국 그것은 사람들이 승마 기술을 보여 주는 인기 있는 방법이 되었다. 수년 후, 한 프랑스인은 이 경기를 기반으로 기계를 만들었다. 그것에는 중앙의 기둥에서 나오는 쇠사슬로 지탱되는 조각된 목마가 있었다. 오늘날의 회전목마는 그의 발명품에서 유래한다.

시간이 흐르자, 회전목마는 단순한 탈것에서 거대한 기계로 진화했다. 그러나 1860년대 미국인들이 회전목마를 만들기 시작하고 나서야 비로소 그것은 예술품이 되었다. 유럽의 회전목마와 달리, 미국의 회전목마는 정교하게 손으로 조각한 말, 사자, 심지어 용까지 있어 아름다웠다. 이때가 회전목마의 전성기였다. 곧, 회전목마는 전국 놀이공원의 중심이 되었다.

그러나 1930년대 대공황 무렵에 회전목마는 인기를 잃게 되었고, 많은 수가 망가지거나 파괴되었다. 그러나 경제가 호전되면서, 회전목마를 만드는 기술도 역시 좋아졌다. 손으로 조각한 목마를 사용하는 대신에, 회전목마를 만드는 사람들은 유리 섬유와 알루미늄을 사용하기 시작했다. 오늘날, 회전목마는 다시 한번 아이들의 필수 놀이기구가 되었다.

어휘 merry-go-round[mérigouràund] 몡 회전목마(= carousel)　amusement park 놀이공원
flashing[flǽʃiŋ] 웹 번쩍거리는　catch one's attention …의 관심을 끌다　innocent[ínəsənt]
몡 무죄인; *순진한, 순수한　ride[raid] 몡 탈것, 놀이기구　start off 출발하다, 시작하다
on horseback 말을 타고　warrior[wɔ́:riər] 몡 전사　carve[ka:rv] 등 (나무·돌 등에) 새기다
[조각하다]　hold up …을 지탱하다　chain[tʃein] 몡 사슬, 쇠줄　pole[poul] 몡 기둥
invention[invénʃən] 몡 발명; *발명품　evolve[iválv] 등 진화하다 (evolution 몡 진화)
work of art 예술품　detailed[ditéild] 웹 상세한　golden age 황금기, 전성기　Great
Depression 대공황　fall out of favor 인기가 떨어지다　fiberglass[fáibərglæs] 몡 유리 섬유
aluminum[əlú:mənəm] 몡 알루미늄　[문제] weapon[wépən] 몡 무기　nobleman[nóublmən]
몡 귀족　preserve[prizə́:rv] 등 보호하다; *보존하다

구문 5행 **It** is hard [**to believe** that *such an innocent children's ride* started off as a training tool for war].
• It은 가주어이고, to believe 이하가 진주어
• such + a(n) + 형용사 + 명사: 그처럼 …한 ~
9행 The Spanish warriors [**who** saw the game] named it *carosella*, *which* means "a little war."
• who 이하는 The Spanish warriors를 수식하는 주격 관계대명사절

8

17행 However, **it was not until** Americans began making carousels in the 1860s **that** they became works of art.
- it is not until … that ~: …해서야 비로소 ~하다

24행 But as the economy got better, **so did the technology for making carousels**.
- so + 동사 + 주어: '…도 또한 그렇다'의 의미로, so가 맨 앞에 나와서 주어와 동사가 도치됨

STRATEGIC ORGANIZER train, horsemanship, machine, details, unwanted

EXPANDING KNOWLEDGE

1 d **2** b

> 당신만의 회전목마의 말을 소유할 수 있다는 사실을 알았는가? 사실 그것들은 인기 있는 수집 품목이다. 회전목마의 말들은 숙련된 예술가에 의해 만들어진 독특한 예술품으로 여겨진다. 대부분의 말들은 일반적으로 색칠되어 나오지만, 어떤 사람들은 자신만의 개성적인 느낌을 주기 위해 자신들의 말에 직접 색칠하는 것을 선호한다. 회전목마의 말은 다양한 장소에서 구입할 수 있다. 요즘은 대부분의 사람들이 온라인으로 찾아보지만, 골동품 상점이나 지역 경매에서도 훌륭한 보물이 발견된다. 말은 종종 아이들의 생일 선물로 주어지기도 하지만, 많은 사람들이 자신의 집에 그저 고풍스러운 모습을 주기 위해 그것들을 구입한다. 어떤 경우에는, 회전목마의 말이 오랜 세월 한 가정에 자리하면서 대대로 전해진다.

어휘 own [oun] 동 소유하다 형 자기 자신의 regard [rigáːrd] 동 …로 여기다 touch [tʌtʃ] 명 만지기; *느낌, 솜씨 purchase [pə́ːrtʃəs] 동 구입하다 a variety of 다양한 treasure [tréʒər] 명 보물 antique [æntíːk] 명 골동품 형 골동품인; 고풍스러운 auction [ɔ́ːkʃən] 명 경매 pass down 전해 주다, 물려주다 generation [dʒènəréiʃən] 명 세대 [문제] collectable [kəléktəbl] 명 수집 가치가 있는 것

구문 2행 Carousel horses are regarded as unique works of art [**created** by skilled artists].
- created 이하는 unique works of art를 수식하는 과거분사구

4행 … some people **prefer to paint** their horses themselves *to give* them their own personal touch.
- prefer: to부정사와 동명사를 모두 목적어로 취할 수 있음
- to give: '…하기 위해'라는 의미로, 목적을 나타내는 부사적 용법의 to부정사

VOCABULARY REVIEW

A **1** warrior **2** generation **3** carve **4** antique
B **1** destroyed **2** evolved **3** innocent **4** goes around **5** pass down   **C** **1** b **2** c

unit 06 SPORTS

pp. 28-31

An Amazing Race

1 c **2** c **3** b **4** They feel as though they are part of a new, special family. **5** c **6** d

> 극한의 모험이나 어려운 도전을 찾고 있다면, 4대 사막 경주가 확실한 선택이다. 그것은 모든 사람에게 열려 있는 세계적인 스포츠 행사이다.

4대 사막 경주는 지구에서 가장 건조하고 가장 덥고 가장 춥고 가장 바람이 많이 부는 곳들을 가로지르는 7일간 250킬로미터 경주 시리즈이다. 4대 사막은 중국의 고비 사막, 칠레의 아타카마 사막, 이집트의 사하라 사막, 그리고 마지막으로 남극대륙이다. 경주의 총 거리는 1,000킬로미터이다. <u>경주 참가자들은 달리면서, 그들은 정신적으로나 육체적으로 자신의 한계를 시험한다.</u> 그러나 그들은 또한 독특한 기후를 경험하고, 아름다운 경치를 즐기며, 고대 문화를 접한다.

주자들은 마실 물과 잠을 잘 장소를 제공받고, 전문 의료진으로 이루어진 팀의 관리를 받는다. 그러나 그들은 지구에서 가장 혹독한 몇몇 기후 조건들을 통과해 달리는 동안 자신의 식량과 장비를 모두 가지고 다녀야 한다. 경주의 끝 무렵에는 가장 빠른 주자와 가장 느린 주자 간에 50시간이 넘는 격차가 생길 수도 있다. 그러나 대부분의 경쟁자들에게 이 경주는 이기고 지는 것 그 이상이다.

4대 사막 경주가 끝날 때쯤에 다양한 문화권에서 와서 많은 각기 다른 언어를 구사하는 주자들은 놀라운 경험을 공유하게 될 것이다. 이 때문에 그들은 마치 새롭고 특별한 가족의 일원인 것처럼 느끼면서 떠나게 될 것이다. 2002년에 4대 사막 경주를 조직한 Mary Gadams는 "이 행사는 언제나 지구에서 가장 놀랄만한 여정 중의 하나로 여겨졌습니다. 저는 누구든지 이 도전을 감행하는 사람은 결코 전과 같지 않을 것이라고 믿습니다."라고 말했다.

어휘 extreme[ikstrí:m] 혱 극도의, 극심한 adventure[ædvéntʃər] 몡 모험 challenge[tʃǽlindʒ]
몡 도전 (challenging 혱 도전적인) obvious[ábviəs] 혱 명백한; *확실한 Antarctica[æntáːrktikə]
몡 남극대륙 scenery[síːnəri] 몡 경치 encounter[inkáuntər] 동 접하다, 마주치다
ancient[éinʃənt] 혱 고대의 monitor[mánətər] 동 감시하다, 관리하다 professional[prəféʃənl]
몡 전문가 equipment[ikwípmənt] 몡 장비, 도구 harsh[haːrʃ] 혱 혹독한 separate[sépərèit]
동 (둘 사이를) 가르다 a wide range of 넓은 범위의, 다양한 remarkable[rimáːrkəbl] 혱 놀랄
만한 [문제] participate[paːrtísəpèit] 동 참가하다 (participant 몡 참가자) limit[límit] 몡 한계
mentally[méntəli] 부 정신적으로 physically[fízikəli] 부 육체적으로 ultimate[ʌ́ltəmət]
혱 궁극적인

구문 10행 The runners are given water **to drink** and places **to sleep**, ….
  • to drink와 to sleep은 각각 앞의 명사 water와 places를 수식하는 형용사적 용법의 to부정사
13행 At the end of the race, more than 50 hours may **separate** the fastest runners
  from the slowest *ones*.
  • separate A from B: A와 B를 가르다
  • ones: runners를 가리키는 대명사
17행 …, the runners, **who** come from a wide range of cultures and speak many
  different languages, *will have shared* an amazing experience.
  • who: the runners를 보충 설명하는 계속적 용법의 주격 관계대명사
  • will have shared: '(그때까지) 계속 …한 것이 될 것이다'의 의미로, 미래 기준 시점까지 계속되는
    상태나 동작을 나타내는 미래완료

STRATEGIC SUMMARY limits, harshest, equipment, experience

EXPANDING KNOWLEDGE

1 b **2** *1)* T *2)* F

나는 어제 내 인생에서 가장 오래 걸었다. 17시간의 연속 도보는 음식을 먹기 위해 잠시 멈출 때에만 중단되었다. 오전 8시에 7킬로미터의 소금 평원을 가로지르는 끔찍한 트레킹으로 행군을 시작했다. 이후에는, 지형이 훨씬 더 편안해져서 굉장히 아름다운 경치 사진을 찍으면서 걸을 수 있게 되었다. 오후 중반에 태양은 몹시 뜨거운 불덩이로 변했다. 다행히도 약간의 구름이 열기를 조금 완화해주었다. 늦은 오후가 되자 해가 지기 시작했다. 나는 더 따뜻한 옷으로 갈아입었고 다른 어떤 생명체도 보지 못한 채 어둠 속에서 몇 시간 동안 도보를 계속했다. 온 사막이 내 차지였다! 걸으면서 나는 내 삶과 미래에 관해 생각했다. 이것이 바로 내가 이 경주에 등록한 이유, 즉 나 자신에 대해 알게 되는 것이다.

어휘   continuous[kəntínjuəs] ⑱ 지속적인   brief[bri:f] ⑱ 짧은   march[ma:rtʃ] ⑲ 행군
horrible[hɔ́:rəbl] ⑱ 끔찍한   trek[trek] ⑲ 트레킹, 오지 여행   plain[plein] ⑲ 평원
terrain[təréin] ⑲ 지형, 지역   stunning[stʌ́niŋ] ⑱ 굉장히 멋진   scorching[skɔ́:rtʃiŋ] ⑱ 몹시
뜨거운   relief[rilí:f] ⑲ 안도; *경감, 완화   to oneself 혼자 (독차지하는)   sign up for …에
등록하다   [문제] self-reflection[sèlfriflékʃən] ⑲ 자아성찰

구문   4행   Afterward, the terrain was much more comfortable, [**allowing** me to walk …].
     • allowing 이하는 연속동작을 나타내는 분사구문(= and it allowed)
   12행   This is exactly (the reason) **why** I signed up for this race ….
     • why: 이유를 나타내는 관계부사로, 앞에 선행사 the reason이 생략되어 있음

VOCABULARY REVIEW

A   **1** extreme   **2** obvious   **3** encounter   **4** monitor
B   **1** participants   **2** separated   **3** organize   **4** continuous   **5** scenery   **C**   **1** b   **2** d

unit 07 FESTIVALS

pp. 32-35

Diwali

1 a   **2** It is the defeat of evil by good and the start of a prosperous new year.   **3** d   **4** a   **5** d
6 1) T   2) F

> 매년 10월 혹은 11월에, 인도 전역의 마을들이 점토로 만들어진 등의 부드러운 불빛으로 밝혀진다. 이것은 디왈리가 돌아왔다는 확실한 표시이다.
>
> 디왈리는 그 나라에서 가장 중요한 축제로, 기독교 세계의 크리스마스와 유사하다. 그 이름은 '점토로 만들어진 등'이라는 뜻의 deepa와 '열'이라는 뜻의 avali라는 두 단어의 합성어에서 유래한다. 당신이 추측하는 것처럼, 빛은 이 축제에서 중요한 역할을 한다.
>
> 디왈리는 본래 한 해의 마지막 추수를 축하하기 위해 힌두교 신자들에 의해 기념되었다. 각기 다른 지역의 힌두교인들은 디왈리의 의미를 설명하기 위해 서로 다른 이야기들을 사용한다. 하지만 한 가지 주제가 늘 존재하는데, 바로 선에 의한 악의 패배와 풍요로운 새해의 시작이다!
>
> 오늘날에는, 모든 종파의 인도인들이 디왈리 행사에 참여한다. 일반적으로 이 행사는 전등, 초, 그리고 꽃으로 만들어진 장식을 붙이고 나서, 가족들을 만나 그들과 잔치를 벌이는 것을 포함한다. 좀 더 구체적으로, 디왈리의 각 5일은 서로 다른 방식으로 기념되어야 한다. 첫 번째 날에, 사람들은 집을 청소하고 축제 용품을 구입한다. 두 번째 날은 집을 장식하는 때이다. 세 번째 날은 주된 축제일로, 이때 가족들이 모여 기도하고, 먹고, 불꽃놀이를 본다. 네 번째 날에, 그들은 선물을 교환한다. 그다음 다섯 번째 날은 전통적으로 형제자매들이 서로의 집을 방문하는 때이다.
>
> 디왈리는 일 년 중 인도를 방문하기에 가장 흥미로운 때 중 하나이다. 무수히 많은 장식은 온 도시를 빛과 색의 폭발로 바꿔 놓는다. 이러한 '빛의 축제'에 참여해 보고 싶지 않은가?

어휘   light[lait] ⑧ 불을 밝히다 ⑲ 빛   clay[klei] ⑲ 점토, 찰흙   significant[signífikənt] ⑱ 중요한
combination[kàmbənéiʃən] ⑲ 결합, 조합(물)   row[rou] ⑲ 열, 줄   assume[əsú:m] ⑧ 추측하다
harvest[há:rvist] ⑲ 추수   theme[θi:m] ⑲ 주제   present[préznt] ⑱ 존재하는   defeat[difí:t]
⑲ 패배   prosperous[práspərəs] ⑱ 번영하는   faith[feiθ] ⑲ 신념; *신앙   decoration[dèkəréiʃən]
⑲ 장식 (decorate ⑧ 장식하다)   feast[fi:st] ⑧ 마음껏 먹다, 잔치에 참여하다   specifically
[spisífikəli] ⑤ 명확하게; *구체적으로 말하면   supply[səplái] ⑲ 공급; *물자, 용품   exchange
[ikstʃéindʒ] ⑧ 교환하다   countless[káuntlis] ⑱ 무수히 많은   explosion[iksplóuʒən] ⑲ 폭발

구문	2행	This is a sure sign [**that** Diwali has come again].
		• that: a sure sign과 동격인 명사절을 이끄는 접속사
	11행	In general, these include **putting up** decorations [*made of* electric lights, candles, and flowers], and then **seeing** family and **feasting** with them.
		• putting up, seeing, feasting은 include의 목적어로 쓰인 동명사(구)
		• made of 이하는 decorations를 수식하는 과거분사구
	16행	The third day is the main holiday, **when** families gather to pray, ….
		• when: the main holiday를 보충 설명하는 계속적 용법의 관계부사
	18행	Then the fifth day is traditionally the time **for brothers and sisters** *to visit* one another's homes.
		• for brothers and sisters: to부정사의 의미상 주어
		• to visit: the time을 수식하는 형용사적 용법의 to부정사

STRATEGIC ORGANIZER   triumph, Happens, harvest, decorate, gifts

EXPANDING KNOWLEDGE

1 a   **2** *1)* F *2)* T

> 40일이 넘는 동안, 사람들은 힌두교의 가장 중요한 축제 중 하나인 Kumbh Mela를 기념한다. 축제 동안 그들은 춤을 추고, 노래를 부르고, 자선 활동을 한다. 하지만 주요 행사는 특정한 날짜에 인도의 신성한 네 개의 강에서 목욕을 하는 것이다. 힌두교도들은 그 강에서 목욕을 하는 것이 이생에서의 자신들의 죄를 용서받게 한다고 믿는다. 이 축제는 사람들을 전 세계에서 인도로 끌어모은다. 그것은 3년마다 열리고, 네 개의 강에서 차례로 개최된다. 그러므로 그 축제는 각 강에서 12년마다 한 번씩 열리고, 이것은 Purna Kumbh Mela라고 불린다. 열두 번의 Purna Kumbh Mela 후에는 Maha Kumbh Mela가 열린다. 가장 최근의 것은 1억 명의 참가자들과 함께 2001년에 열렸다.

어휘	charity[tʃǽrəti] 명 자선 bathe[beið] 통 (몸을) 씻다 sacred[séikrid] 형 신성한
	specific[spisífik] 형 구체적인; *특정한 sin[sin] 명 (종교·도덕상의) 죄(악) forgive[fərgív]
	통 용서하다 attract[ətrǽkt] 통 끌어모으다 last[læst] 형 마지막의; *가장 최근의

구문	4행	Hindus believe that bathing in the rivers **allows** their sins of this life **to be forgiven**.
		• allow + 목적어 + to-v: …가 ~하게 하다
	7행	It takes place every three years, and the four rivers **take turns holding** it.
		• take turns v-ing: 차례로 …하다

VOCABULARY REVIEW

A   **1** prosperous   **2** feast   **3** decorate   **4** forgive
B   **1** harvest   **2** bathe   **3** take part in   **4** combination   **5** exchange   **C**   **1** c   **2** b

unit
08 ORIGINS

pp. 36-39

★*The Best Man and Bridesmaids*

1 b   **2** d   **3** He protected the groom during and after the wedding.   **4** b   **5** d   **6** *1)* T *2)* T

결혼식의 주인공은 누구일까? 물론, 신부와 신랑이다. 그런데 현대 결혼식은 다른 중요한 사람들을 포함한다. 신랑 측에는, 신랑 들러리가 있고 신부 측에는 신부 들러리가 있다. 이 사람들은 결혼식 동안 신부와 신랑을 지원하고 식을 준비하는 것을 도와준다. 그러나 그들의 원래 역할은 훨씬 더 어려웠다.

신랑 들러리의 전통은 초기 게르만 시대로 거슬러 올라간다. 이 시대에는 결혼이 항상 낭만적인 것은 아니었다. 남자는 종종 이웃 마을에서 여자를 납치해 그녀에게 결혼을 강요했었다! 이것은 하기가 어려워, 예비 신랑은 도와줄 사람을 필요로 했다. 그래서 그는 아는 사람 중에서 그가 결혼하도록 도와줄 '최적의 사람'을 선택했다. 결혼식을 하는 동안과 그 이후에 신랑을 보호하는 일 역시 신랑 들러리가 할 일이었다. 만약 신부의 가족이 그녀를 구하러 오면, 틀림없이 싸움이 생길 것이었다.

신부 들러리는 거의 신랑 들러리만큼이나 오랫동안 존재해 왔다. 고대 로마에서는 법에 열 명의 사람들이 결혼식에 증인으로 서야 한다고 되어 있었다. 그렇지 않으면, 그것은 합법적인 것이 아니었다. 그래서 신부의 친구들과 가족이 증인으로 결혼식에 참석했다. 후에 신부 들러리는 다른 역할을 수행하기 시작했다. 사람들은 신부와 신랑에게 불행을 안겨주기 위해 악령들이 결혼식에 온다고 생각했다. 신부 들러리는 누가 결혼하는지 혼령들이 알지 못하도록 신부의 것과 똑같은 드레스를 입고 악령을 속여야 했다. 오늘날 신부 들러리들은 여전히 신부와 비슷하게 옷을 입어 혼령들을 속인다!

어휘　bride[braid] 몡 신부　groom[gru:m] 몡 신랑　best man 신랑 들러리　bridesmaid [bráidzmèid] 몡 신부 들러리　arrange[əréindʒ] 통 정하다, 준비하다　ceremony[sérəmòuni] 몡 식, 의식　date back to …까지 거슬러 올라가다　era[íərə] 몡 시대, 시기　romantic[rouмǽntik] 혱 낭만적인　capture[kǽptʃər] 통 붙잡다　neighboring[néibəriŋ] 혱 이웃의, 근처의　force[fɔ:rs] 통 강요하다　assist[əsíst] 통 돕다　rescue[réskju:] 통 구출하다　witness[wítnis] 통 (증인으로서) …에 입회하다 몡 증인　legal[lí:ɡəl] 혱 합법적인　function[fʌ́ŋkʃən] 몡 기능, 역할　be supposed to-v …하기로 되어 있다　trick[trik] 통 속이다　identical[aidéntikəl] 혱 동일한　fool[fu:l] 통 속이다　[문제] aggressive[əgrésiv] 혱 공격적인　hostile[hástl] 혱 적대적인　mutual[mjú:tʃuəl] 혱 상호간의

구문　13행　During this era, marriage was **not always** romantic.
• not always: '항상 …한 것은 아니다'라는 의미의 부분부정
16행　Thus, he chose the "best man" [(who(m)[that]) **he knew**] to *help* him *get* married.
• he knew 앞에 the "best man"을 선행사로 하는 목적격 관계대명사가 생략되어 있음
• help + 목적어 + 동사원형: …가 ～하도록 돕다
16행　**It** was also the job of the best man [**to protect** the groom …].
• It은 가주어이고, to protect 이하가 진주어
25행　… to the bride's **so that** the spirits wouldn't know [*who* was getting married].
• so that: …하기 위하여
• who 이하는 '의문사(주어) +동사' 어순의 간접의문문으로, 동사 know의 목적어 역할을 함

STRATEGIC ORGANIZER　arrange, capture, safe, witnesses, identically

EXPANDING KNOWLEDGE

1 d　**2** d

북미에서는 여성이 결혼할 때, 종종 여러 명의 신부 들러리를 선택한다. 그리고 이 여성들 중 오직 한 명만이 대표 신부 들러리가 되는데, 그녀는 보통 신부의 절친한 친구이거나 자매이다. 그녀는 일반적으로 몇 가지 책임을 맡는다. 결혼식에 참석하는 것 <u>외</u>에 그녀는 청첩장을 보내는 것부터 드레스를 고르는 것까지 모든 것에서 종종 신부를 도와준다. 결혼식 날에, 대표 신부 들러리는 신부에게 실질적이고도 정서적인 지원을 해준다. 그녀는 결혼식 동안 신랑의 결혼반지를 보관하기도 한다. 또한, 그녀는 결혼식의 법적 증인이 되어달라고 요청받을 수도 있다. 피로연에서 대표 신부 들러리는 대개 신혼부부를 위한 건배를 제안한다.

어휘   maid of honor (신부 들러리 중 결혼을 하지 않은) 대표 들러리   reception[risépʃən] 뗑 리셉션, 피로연
        toast[toust] 뗑 건배   newlywed[njú:liwèd] 뗑 (pl.) 신혼부부   [문제] regardless of …에 관계없이
        accompany[əkʌ́mpəni] 뙁 동반하다, 동행하다

구문   2행   … will be the maid of honor, **who** is usually the bride's best friend or sister.
             • who: the maid of honor를 보충 설명하는 계속적 용법의 주격 관계대명사

VOCABULARY REVIEW

A   *1* legal *2* neighboring *3* arrange *4* rescue
B   *1* bride *2* ancient *3* capture *4* fight *5* identical   C *1* a *2* d

unit 09 LITERATURE

pp. 40-43

The Wizard of Oz

1 c *2* She pulled open the cellar door and ran down the stairs. *3* d *4* c *5* b *6* *1)* F *2)* F

> 도로시는 엠 아주머니가 설거지를 하는 동안 그녀의 개 토토와 놀고 있었다. 갑자기 헨리 아저씨가 놀란 표정을 하고 부엌으로 급히 들어왔다.
>
> "토네이도가 오고 있어."라고 그는 소리쳤다. "지하실로 내려가!" 엠 아주머니는 지하실 문을 당겨 열고 계단을 뛰어 내려갔다. 도로시도 따라가기 시작했으나, 바로 그때 토토가 그녀의 팔에서 뛰어나와 달아나 버렸다. 도로시가 그를 잡을 수 있었을 때, 이상한 일이 일어나고 있었다.
>
> 처음엔 집이 흔들리기 시작했고, 그다음 회전하기 시작했다. 그리고 마침내 그것은 서서히 공중으로 떠오르기 시작했다. 그들은 토네이도의 중심에 있었다! 집은 토네이도의 꼭대기까지 올라가서 폭풍 치는 바다 위의 배처럼 흔들리며 그곳에 머물러 있었다. 토토는 겁에 질려 짖어댔지만, 도로시는 그를 팔에 단단히 안고 다음에 무슨 일이 일어날지 보려고 기다렸다.
>
> 그들은 수 마일을 이동해 온 것이 틀림없었다. 바람이 너무 시끄럽게 불어서 도로시는 아무것도 들을 수가 없었다. 집은 절대 다시 내려가지 않을 것처럼 보였다. 그리고 만약 내려간다 해도 무슨 일이 일어날까? 집이 박살 나 산산조각이 날까? 도로시는 알 수 없었다. 그러고 나서 몇 시간이 지났고 아무 일도 일어나지 않았다. 천천히 그녀의 두려움이 사라지기 시작했다. 도로시는 걱정을 그만두고 침착하게 기다리면서 무슨 일이 일어나는지 보기로 결심했다.
>
> 마침내, 그녀는 자신의 침실로 걸어갔고 침대로 올라갔다. 비록 집이 흔들리고 바람은 윙윙거리고 있었지만, 도로시는 눈을 감자마자 빠르게 잠들었다.

어휘   alarmed[əlάːrmd] 뗑 놀란   tornado[tɔːrnéidou] 뗑 토네이도   yell[jel] 뙁 소리치다   cellar
        [sélər] 뗑 지하실   pull open 당겨서 열다   spin[spin] 뙁 돌다, 회전하다   rock[rak] 뙁 흔들리다
        stormy[stɔ́ːrmi] 뗑 폭풍우가 몰아치는   bark[baːrk] 뙁 짖다   tightly[táitli] 뮌 단단히, 꼭
        smash[smæʃ] 뙁 박살 내다   resolve[rizάlv] 뙁 해결하다; *결심하다   calmly[kάːmli] 뮌 침착하게
        sway[swei] 뙁 흔들리다   howl[haul] 뙁 울부짖다; *(바람이) 윙윙거리다   [문제] sweep away …을
        쓸어내다, 휩쓸어 가다   sorrowful[sάrəfəl] 뗑 슬픈   astonished[əstάniʃt] 뗑 놀란

구문   7행   …, **something strange** was happening.
             • something strange: -thing으로 끝나는 대명사는 형용사가 뒤에서 수식함
        11행   … and remained there, [**rocking** like a ship on a stormy sea].
             • rocking 이하는 동시동작을 나타내는 분사구문
        15행   They **must have traveled** for miles and miles.
             • must have v-ed: '…했음에 틀림없다'의 의미로, 과거에 대한 강한 추측을 나타냄

15행 The wind was blowing **so** loudly **that** Dorothy **couldn't** hear a thing.
  • so … that + 주어 + can't ~: 너무 …해서 ~할 수 없다
16행 It seemed **as if** the house **would** never come back down.
  • as if + 가정법 과거: 마치 …인 것처럼

STRATEGIC SUMMARY tornado, cellar, blew, scared, asleep

EXPANDING KNOWLEDGE

1 c **2** *1)* T *2)* F

당신은 '저 높이 무지개 너머 어딘가에 …'로 시작하는 노래를 아마도 잘 알고 있을 것이다. 제목이 'Over the Rainbow'인 이 노래가 *오즈의 마법사*라는 1939년 영화에서 나온 것을 알고 있었는가? 주인공인 도로시는 색다르고 흥미진진한 세상에 가 보는 것을 꿈꾸는, 작은 마을에 사는 호기심 많은 소녀이다. 영화에서 그녀는 무지개 너머에 있는 아름다운 곳을 꿈꾸면서 이 노래를 부른다. 도로시 역을 맡았던 여배우이자 가수 Judy Garland가 영화에서 직접 이 노래를 불렀다. 노래 'Over the Rainbow'는 큰 인기를 얻었고, 그해 아카데미 주제가상을 받았다. 이후, 이 노래는 수없이 많은 음악가에 의해 불렸고 고전이 되었다.

어휘 somewhere[sʌ́mhwɛər] 뤼 어딘가에 curious[kjúəriəs] 혱 호기심 많은 locate[lóukeit] 동 …에 두다[놓다] actress[ǽktris] 명 여배우 classic[klǽsik] 명 고전, 명작

구문 4행 …, Dorothy, is a curious girl from a small town [**who** dreams of …].
  • who 이하는 a curious girl을 수식하는 주격 관계대명사절
  5행 In the movie, she sings this song [**while dreaming** of a beautiful place *located over the rainbow*].
  • while dreaming 이하는 때를 나타내는 분사구문으로, 의미를 명확하게 하기 위해 접속사를 생략하지 않음
  • located 이하는 a beautiful place를 수식하는 과거분사구
  10행 Since then, this song **has been sung** by countless musicians ….
  • has been sung: '…되어 왔다'라는 의미의 현재완료 수동태

VOCABULARY REVIEW

A **1** sway **2** cellar **3** howl **4** classic
B **1** curious **2** bark **3** yelled **4** smashed **5** tightly   C **1** b **2** d

unit
10 FOOD   pp. 44-47

★Beer

1 b **2** b **3** c **4** Because specific regions and countries make beer with different ingredients and methods. **5** d **6** *1)* F *2)* T

거품이 있는 노르스름한 액체를 상상해보라. 이것은 당신이 생각하고 있었을지 모르는 탄산음료가 아니다. 이것은 8,000년의 역사를 가진 알코올음료인 맥주이다.

기원전 6,000년경, 수메르인들은 보리나 밀로 만든 빵을 먹었다. 어느 날, 약간의 빵이 아마도 엎질러진 물이나 비로 젖었다. 이 젖은 빵은 공기 중에 있는 자연 효모균의 영향을 받았다. 곧 빵은 거품으로 뒤덮였고, 너무 푹 젖어서

그것은 씹는다기보다는 마실 수 있었다. 그것을 마신 사람들은 그 달콤하고 기분 좋은 맛을 좋아했고, 먹기 위해 '액체 빵'을 만들기 시작했다. 이것이 맥주의 탄생이었다.

고대 수메르와 이집트에서는 17에서 20가지의 서로 다른 종류의 맥주가 만들어졌다고 한다. 여자들은 밀로 만들어진 맥주에 꿀이나 계피를 첨가하여 마셨고, 남자들은 보리로 만든 쓴 맥주를 즐겼다. 고대 정부는 맥주 제조를 관리했고, 매일 모든 시민에게 일정량을 주었다. 또한, 약이나 약초, 향신료와 혼합한 맥주는 배탈을 치료하는 데 사용되었다. (음식은 냉장될 수 없었기 때문에 종종 상했고, 이는 복통과 메스꺼움을 유발했다.) 맥주 제조업 종사자들은 매우 존경을 받았고, 성직자들과 마찬가지로 그들은 전쟁 중에 군에 복무할 필요가 없었다.

그때 이래로, 맥주 제조는 여러 사회에서 인기를 누렸다. 그것은 중세 시대에 유럽 전역으로 퍼졌지만, 오직 부유한 사람들만이 그것을 즐길 수 있었다. 그러나 오늘날 맥주는 또다시 모든 계층 사람들의 음료가 되었다. 특정 지역과 국가들이 서로 다른 재료와 방법으로 맥주를 만들며, 현재 셀 수 없이 많은 종류가 나와 있다.

어휘 yellowish[jélouiʃ] 형 노르스름한   liquid[líkwid] 명 액체 형 액체의   bubble[bʌ́bl] 명 거품   alcoholic[æ̀lkəhɔ́ːlik] 형 술의, 알코올이 든   beverage[bévəridʒ] 명 음료   barley[báːrli] 명 보리   wheat[hwiːt] 명 밀   yeast[jiːst] 명 이스트, 효모균   soaked[soukt] 형 흠뻑 젖은   chew[tʃuː] 동 씹다   flavor[fléivər] 명 풍미, 맛   consumption[kənsʌ́mpʃən] 명 소비   cinnamon[sínəmən] 명 계피   bitter[bítər] 형 쓴   herb[əːrb] 명 허브, 약초   spice[spais] 명 양념, 향신료   refrigerate[rifrídʒərèit] 동 냉장하다   nausea[nɔ́ːziə] 명 메스꺼움   priest[priːst] 명 사제, 성직자   serve[səːrv] 동 제공하다; *근무[복무]하다   class[klæs] 명 학급; *계층   method[méθəd] 명 방법   currently[kə́ːrəntli] 부 현재, 지금   variety[vəráiəti] 명 다양성; *종류   available[əvéiləbl] 형 이용할 수 있는   [문제] liquor[líkər] 명 술

구문   1행   This is not soda as you **may have been** thinking.
   • may have v-ed: '…이었을지도 모른다'의 의미로, 과거 사실에 대한 불확실한 추측을 나타냄
   3행   Around 6000 B.C., the Sumerians ate bread [**made of** barley or wheat].
   • made of 이하는 bread를 수식하는 과거분사구
   6행   … and became **so** soaked **that** it could be drunk rather than chewed.
   • so … that ~: 너무 …해서 ~하다
   9행   **It** is said [**that** 17 to 20 different kinds of beer were made …].
   • It은 가주어이고, that 이하가 진주어
   10행   Women drank beer made from wheat **with** honey or cinnamon **added**, ….
   • with + 명사 + v-ed: '…가 ~된 채로'라는 의미의 분사구문으로, 명사와 분사가 수동 관계일 때 과거분사를 씀
   22행   …, and currently there are countless varieties [(which are) **available**].
   • available 앞에 '주격 관계대명사 + be동사'가 생략되어 있음

STRATEGIC SUMMARY   drinkable, bitter, important, serve, enjoy

EXPANDING KNOWLEDGE

1 d   **2** 1) T 2) T

1516년, 지금의 독일에 사는 바이에른 귀족 두 명은 맥주는 보리, 물, 그리고 홉으로만 만들 수 있다고 명시한 법을 만들었다. 이는 결국 맥주 순수령으로 알려지게 되었다. 하지만 맥주를 순수하게 유지하는 것이 본래 의도는 아니었다. 그것은 사실 맥주 제조자들이 밀이나 호밀과 같은 더 귀중한 곡물들을 사용하지 못하게 하려고 작성되었다. 맥주를 주조하는 곡물을 보리로 제한함으로써, 그 법은 그러한 귀중한 곡물들이 제빵업자용으로 비축되도록 보장해주었다. 그러나 제2차 세계대전 후에, 그 법은 독일 맥주의 질을 홍보하기 위한 마케팅 수단이 되었다. 이 법 덕분에 독일 맥주는 현재 우월한 품질과 맛의 일관성으로 전 세계에 알려져 있다.

어휘 nobleman[nóublmən] 명 귀족   state[steit] 동 명시하다, 쓰다   hop[hap] 명 (pl.) 홉(맥주의 원료)

16

eventually[ivéntʃuəli] 彤 결국　intent[intént] 阁 의도　grain[grein] 阁 곡물　ensure[inʃúər]
통 보장하다　reserve[rizə́ːrv] 통 남겨두다, 보존하다　promote[prəmóut] 통 촉진하다; *홍보하다
superior[səpíəriər] 형 우수한, 우월한　consistency[kənsístənsi] 阁 일관성

구문　1행　... noblemen in **what** is now Germany made a law [*stating* that beer ...].
　　　　　• what: '… 하는 것'의 의미로, 선행사를 포함하는 관계대명사(= the thing which)
　　　　　• stating 이하는 a law를 수식하는 현재분사구
　　　4행　It was actually written to **stop** beer makers **from using** more valuable grains, ...
　　　　　• stop + 목적어 + from v-ing: …가 ～하는 것을 막다

VOCABULARY REVIEW

A　**1** consistency　**2** nobleman　**3** liquid　**4** chew
B　**1** citizens　**2** consumption　**3** ingredients　**4** beverages　**5** nausea　　**C**　**1** a　**2** c

PEOPLE

pp. 48-51

Da Vinci's Kitchen

1 d　**2** c　**3** b　**4** He believed that eating small amounts of food was good for a person's health.　**5** b　**6** *1)* F　*2)* T

1981년, *El Codex Romanoff*라는 제목의 책이 러시아의 Hermitage 국립 미술관에서 발견되었다. 이 책은 식사 예절, 식습관, 요리법, 주방 관리, 그리고 새로운 조리 도구와 같은 음식 문화에 관한 정보를 담고 있었다. 1490년대에 쓰인 이 책은 레오나르도 다빈치에 의해 저술되었다는 것이 확인되었다.

요리는 르네상스 시대의 천재 화가이자 과학자, 발명가 그리고 사상가였던 다빈치에게 특별한 취미였다. 요리에 대한 그의 열정은 단순한 취미 이상이었다. 그는 부업으로 이탈리아의 Sforza 성에서 연회 지배인으로 30년간 일했다. 그는 또한 주방에서는 주방장이었고, 위대한 화가 보티첼리와 함께 음식점을 운영했다.

뛰어난 발명가로서 그는 여러 주방 도구를 고안했다. 그의 파스타 면 만드는 기계, 삶은 달걀을 자르는 도구, 포크, 냅킨 건조기, 마늘 으깨는 기구, 후추 가는 기구의 디자인을 보면, 요즘 사용되는 도구와 이들 디자인의 유사점을 볼 수 있다.

다빈치는 또한 적은 양의 음식을 먹는 것이 개인의 건강에 좋다고 믿었다. 그는 당근 네 조각과 함께 멸치 단 한 마리를 내는 것과 같은 요리를 제공함으로써 이를 자신의 음식점 메뉴에 적용했다. 그러나 그 당시 사람들은 그의 혁신적인 주방 도구나 새로운 요리법에 관심이 없었다. 약 500년 후에야 그것들은 유용성과 창의성을 인정받고 있다. 레오나르도 다빈치는 진정으로 시대를 앞서 간 다재다능한 천재였다.

어휘　dining etiquette 식사 예절　confirm[kənfəːrm] 통 확인해주다　author[ɔ́ːθər] 통 저술하다,
　　쓰다　genius[dʒíːnjəs] 阁 천재　passion[pǽʃən] 阁 열정　banquet[bǽŋkwit] 阁 연회　on
　　the side 부업으로　outstanding[àutstǽndiŋ] 형 뛰어난　boiled[bɔild] 형 삶은　slicer[sláisər]
　　阁 얇게 자르는 기구　garlic[gáːrlik] 阁 마늘　crusher[krʌ́ʃər] 으깨는 도구　grinder[gráindər]
　　阁 가는 도구　similarity[sìməlǽrəti] 阁 유사점　apply[əplái] 통 신청하다; *쓰다, 적용하다
　　anchovy[ǽntʃouvi] 阁 멸치　innovative[ínəvèitiv] 형 혁신적인　recognize[rékəgnàiz]
　　통 알아보다; *인정하다　multi-talented[mʌltitǽləntid] 형 다재다능한　[문제] enthusiasm
　　[inθúːziæzm] 阁 열정, 열의　behave[bihéiv] 통 행동하다; *예의 바르게 행동하다　be concerned
　　with …와 관계가 있다　appreciate[əpríːʃièit] 통 진가를 알아보다, 인정하다　comparable to …와
　　비슷한, …와 비교할 만한

구문　4행　**It** was confirmed [**that** this book, (which was) *written* in the 1490s, was authored by Leonardo da Vinci].

· It은 가주어이고, that 이하가 진주어

· written 앞에 '주격 관계대명사 + be동사'가 생략되어 있음

11행　[**Looking** at his designs for a pasta-making machine], …, one can see ….

· Looking 이하는 조건을 나타내는 분사구문(= If one looks at …)

22행　Only about 500 years later **are they** being recognized ….

· are they: 부사구(Only about 500 years later)가 문장 앞에 와서 주어와 동사가 도치됨

STRATEGIC SUMMARY　discovered, recipes, interested, designed, popular

EXPANDING KNOWLEDGE

1 b　**2** 1) F　2) T

> 과학자들은 최근에 살을 빼고 기분을 더 좋아지게 하는 데 도움을 줄 수 있는 식이요법을 발견했다. 이것은 레오나르도 다빈치의 지중해식 식단에 기반을 둔 것이다. 기본적으로, 각 식사는 통 곡물 1과 단백질 2, 채소 3의 비율을 포함해야 한다. 그 식단은 오메가3와 같은 좋은 지방을 포함하기 때문에 특히 건강에 좋은데, 오메가3는 올리브유나 생선에서 발견된다. 그 연구는 매일 와인 한 잔을 마시는 것이 혈압을 낮추는 데 도움이 될 수 있다는 것도 밝혀냈다. 다빈치 식단의 인기는 다빈치 시대에 따랐던 많은 건강 트렌드가 오늘날에도 여전히 인기 있다는 것을 보여준다.

어휘　essentially[isénʃəli] 🔼 본질적으로　part[paːrt] 명 부분; *(혼합 등의) 비율　whole grain 통 곡물　protein[próutiːn] 명 단백질　lower[lóuər] 통 낮추다　blood pressure 혈압　trend[trend] 명 유행, 트렌드　[문제] keep in shape 건강을 유지하다

구문　5행　… it includes good fats such as omega-3, **which** is found in olive oil and fish.

· which: omega-3를 보충 설명하는 계속적 용법의 주격 관계대명사(= and it)

9행　… many of the health trends [**followed** in the time of da Vinci] *remain popular* today.

· followed 이하는 many of the health trends를 수식하는 과거분사구

· remain + 형용사: 여전히 …이다

VOCABULARY REVIEW

A　**1** grain　**2** apply　**3** passion　**4** grinder

B　**1** appreciated　**2** banquet　**3** innovative　**4** trends　**5** similarities　**C**　**1** c　**2** b

unit 12 BIOLOGY

pp. 52-55

*Earworms

1 b　**2** c　**3** d　**4** c　**5** They usually have simple melodies and repetitive lyrics.　**6** 1) F　2) T

> 어느 날 아침, 당신은 라디오를 켜고 당신이 매우 좋아하는 밴드가 그들의 최신곡을 부르는 것을 듣는다. 학교로 가는 버스에서 여전히 당신의 머릿속에 그 노래가 들린다. 심지어 수업 시간에도 계속 반복해서 들린다. 왜 이런 일이 일어나고 있는 것일까? 전문가에 따르면 당신은 귀벌레에 감염된 것이다.
>
> 　당신은 어떤 이상한 생명체가 당신의 귀 안에서 기어 다니는 것을 상상할지도 모른다. 그러나 사실 귀벌레는 당신의 머릿속에 들어가 뇌에 일종의 '가려움증'을 유발하는 노래의 일부이다. 귀벌레가 생기면, 청각 피질이라고

불리는 뇌의 일부분이 노래의 나머지를 채우려 한다. 그래서 당신의 뇌는 그 노래가 끝난 지 한참 후에도 계속 '노래하는' 것이다. 그리고 한번 '긁기' 시작하면 멈추기 힘들다. 아무도 무엇이 귀벌레를 유발하는지는 정확히 알지 못한다. 어떤 사람들은 그것이 생각을 멈추려 애쓰는 것과 같다고 생각한다. 예를 들어, 누군가 당신에게 분홍 코끼리에 대해 생각하지 말라고 한다면, 당신은 그렇게 하지 않는 것이 불가능하다는 것을 알게 될 것이다. 그것은 노래에도 같은 방식으로 작용할 수 있다. 다른 사람들은 귀벌레가 뇌가 할 일이 없을 때 뇌를 바쁘게 유지하는 간단한 방법이라고 생각한다.

어떤 종류의 노래가 귀벌레를 유발할 가능성이 가장 클까? 모든 사람이 다르지만, 그 노래들에는 보통 단순한 멜로디와 반복되는 가사가 있다. 진짜 노래일 필요까지도 없다. 광고나 심지어는 휴대전화 벨 소리도 귀벌레를 유발할 수 있다.

귀벌레가 생긴다 해도 당신은 그것에 대해 걱정할 필요가 없다. 사실, 당신은 음악을 귀뿐만 아니라 뇌로도 듣는데, 그것은 지극히 자연스러운 것이다. 그러니 그저 음악을 즐겨라!

어휘
infect[infékt] ⑧ 감염시키다　　creature[kríːtʃər] ⑲ 생명체, 생물　　crawl[krɔːl] ⑧ 기어 다니다
itch[itʃ] ⑲ 간지러움　　section[sékʃən] ⑲ 부분　　fill in 채우다　　scratch[skrætʃ] ⑧ 긁다
repetitive[ripétətiv] ⑲ 반복적인　　lyric[lírik] ⑲ (pl.) 가사　　commercial[kəmə́ːrʃəl] ⑲ 광고
ringtone[ríŋtòun] ⑲ 벨 소리, 신호음　　perfectly[pə́ːrfiktli] ⑨ 완전히, 지극히　　[문제] symptom
[símptəm] ⑲ 징후, 증상　　get stuck 꼼짝 못하게 되다　　frequently[fríːkwəntli] ⑨ 자주, 빈번히
criticize[krítəsàiz] ⑧ 비판하다, 비평하다　　analyze[ǽnəlàiz] ⑧ 분석하다
phenomenon[finámənən] ⑲ 현상　　idle[áidl] ⑧ 하는 일 없이 지내다

구문
7행　You might **imagine** some strange creature **crawling** inside your ear.
　　• imagine + 목적어 + v-ing: …가 ~하는 것을 상상하다

12행　No one is sure exactly [**what** causes earworms].
　　• what 이하는 '의문사(주어) + 동사' 어순의 간접의문문

13행　…, if someone **tells** you not **to think** about pink elephants, you will find *it* is impossible *not to* (think about pink elephants).
　　• tell + 목적어 + to-v: …에게 ~하라고 말하다[명령하다]
　　• it은 가목적어이고, not to가 진목적어
　　• not to 뒤에 반복되는 부분인 think about pink elephants가 생략됨

15행　… is a simple way **to keep** the brain *busy* when it has nothing **to do**.
　　• to keep과 to do는 각각 앞의 a simple way와 nothing을 수식하는 형용사적 용법의 to부정사
　　• keep + 목적어 + 형용사: …을 ~하게 유지하다

23행　…, you listen to music with **not only** your ears **but also** your brain, *which* is ….
　　• not only A but also B: A뿐만 아니라 B도
　　• which: 앞의 절을 선행사로 하는 계속적 용법의 주격 관계대명사

STRATEGIC SUMMARY　repeat, worm, stuck, happens, simple

EXPANDING KNOWLEDGE

1 c　**2** *1)* T　*2)* T

큰 조개껍데기를 귀에 갖다 대면, 당신은 굽이치는 파도소리를 들을지도 모른다. 조개껍데기가 어떻게 바닷소리를 내는지 궁금했던 적이 있는가? 사실 그것들은 소리를 내지 않는다. 그 소리가 바다의 울부짖는 소리처럼 들릴지도 모르지만, 그것은 사실 항상 당신의 주변에 있는 작은 소리에 불과하다. 어떻게 이런 일이 생길까? 그것은 조개껍데기의 모양과 관련 있다. 조개껍데기의 내부는 마치 기타의 내부처럼 비어 있다. 그리고 또 기타와 마찬가지로 이 빈 공간이 소리를 훨씬 더 크게 만드는 것이다. 그래서 조개껍데기를 귀에 댈 때마다, 당신은 실제로 주위의 모든 작은 소리가 조개껍데기에 의해 보다 커진 것을 듣고 있는 것이다.

seashell[síːʃèl] 명 조개껍데기   roar[rɔːr] 명 (바람 · 바다 등이) 울부짖는 듯한 소리 동 (바람 · 파도 등이) 굉음을 내다   have to do with …와 관련이 있다   hollow[hálou] 형 (속이) 빈

구문   3행   ..., but they are actually just the small sounds [**that** are around you all the time].
· that 이하는 the small sounds를 수식하는 주격 관계대명사절

7행   ..., this empty area **makes** sounds *much* **louder**.
· make + 목적어 + 형용사: …을 ～하게 하다
· much: '훨씬'의 의미로, 비교급을 강조하는 부사

8행   ..., you're really **hearing** all the little noises around you **being** made louder by the shell.
· 지각동사(hear) + 목적어 + v-ing: …가 ～하고 있는 것을 듣다

VOCABULARY REVIEW
A   **1** crawl   **2** rest   **3** itch   **4** roar
B   **1** infected   **2** shape   **3** wonder   **4** repetitive   **5** lyrics   C   **1** b   **2** b

13 ANIMALS
pp. 56-59

★Dog Vision
1 c   **2** b   **3** d   **4** It helps them see more of their surroundings, not just what is directly in front of them.   **5** a   **6** 1) T 2) F

개에게 세상이 어떻게 보이는지 궁금했던 적이 있는가? 아마도 신발은 재미있는 장난감처럼 보이고, 뼈는 맛있는 식사와 닮았을 것이다. 사실, 인간의 시력과 개의 시력에는 몇 가지 큰 차이점이 있다.

인간들은 그들이 하는 거의 모든 일에 있어서 시력에 의존하지만, 개들은 다르다. 개들은 듣고 냄새 맡기를 매우 잘할 수 있다. 그래서 시력이 우리만큼 좋을 필요가 없다. 사실 인간의 시력은 개의 시력보다 다섯 배 더 좋다. 개는 또한 우리보다 적은 수의 색을 식별한다. 개들은 녹색과 파란색, 또는 빨간색과 노란색을 구별하지 못한다. 개에게 세상은 거의 파란색과 노란색을 띠고 있다. 또 하나의 큰 차이점은 우리의 눈은 앞을 향하고 있는 반면, 개의 눈은 머리의 양쪽 면에 있다는 것이다. 이 때문에 개는 거리 감각이 훨씬 더 나쁘다. 이는 개들이 사물이 얼마나 가깝거나 멀리 있는지 쉽게 구분할 수 없음을 의미한다.

그러나 개는 시력에 있어서 몇 가지 이점을 가지고 있다. 우선 첫째로, 눈의 위치가 개의 바로 앞에 있는 것뿐만 아니라 주변을 더 많이 보는 데 도움이 된다는 것이다. 더욱이, 개는 눈 뒤쪽에 어둠 속에서 우리보다 훨씬 더 잘 볼 수 있게 해주는 특수한 표면을 갖고 있다. 그리고 개들은 먼 곳의 움직임을 보는 데에도 훨씬 더 뛰어나다. 이런 모든 특징들은 개가 훌륭한 사냥꾼이 될 수 있게 해준다.

그것을 생각한다면, 인간이 개보다 더 잘 본다고 말하는 것은 별로 타당하지 않다. 개들은 그저 우리와 다르게 사물을 보는 것뿐이라고 말하는 것이 더 정확하다.

어휘   vision[víʒən] 명 시력   rely on …에 의지하다   extremely[ikstríːmli] 부 극히, 극단적으로   distinguish[distíŋgwiʃ] 동 구별하다, 식별하다   tell[tel] 동 말하다; *구별하다   shade[ʃeid] 명 그늘; *색조   forward[fɔ́ːrwərd] 부 앞으로   depth perception 거리[깊이] 감각   when it comes to …에 관해서   surroundings[səráundiŋz] 명 (pl.) 주변, 환경   directly[diréktli] 부 바로   surface[sə́ːrfis] 명 표면   fair[fɛər] 형 공정한; *타당한   accurate[ǽkjurət] 형 정확한   [문제] discriminate[diskrímənèit] 동 식별하다, 분간하다

구문   1행   **Have** you ever **wondered** [*how* the world looks to a dog]?

- Have wondered: '…한 적이 있다'의 의미로, 경험을 나타내는 현재완료
- how 이하는 '의문사 + 주어 + 동사' 어순의 간접의문문으로, 동사 wondered의 목적어 역할을 함

7행 They cannot **tell** green **from** blue or (tell) *red **from** yellow*.
- tell A from B: A와 B를 구별하다
- red from yellow 앞에 반복되는 동사 tell이 생략되어 있음

13행 …, the position of their eyes **helps** them **see** more of their surroundings, not just *what* is directly in front of them.
- help + 목적어 + 동사원형: …가 ~하도록 돕다
- what: '…하는 것'의 의미로, 선행사를 포함하는 관계대명사(= the thing which)

14행 …, dogs have a special surface in the back of their eyes [**that** *lets* them *see* in the dark **much** better than we *can* (see in the dark)].
- that 이하는 a special surface를 수식하는 주격 관계대명사절
- 사역동사(let) + 목적어 + 동사원형: …가 ~하게 하다
- much: '훨씬'의 의미로, 비교급을 강조하는 부사
- can 뒤에 반복되는 부분인 see in the dark가 생략되어 있음

STRATEGIC ORGANIZER sides, colors, positioning, surface, distance

EXPANDING KNOWLEDGE

1 b **2** d

당신의 개가 길 건너편에서 당신을 향해 달려오고 있다고 상상해보라. 당신은 개가 당신의 외양만을 근거로 당신을 알아볼 것이라 생각할지도 모른다. 그러나 그것은 사실이 아니다. 사실 개는 움직임이 없는 물체는 별로 잘 볼 수 없다. 그렇다면 개가 어떻게 당신인지 알까? 개는 냄새나 목소리 외에도 당신의 고유한 몸짓을 근거로 당신을 알아볼 수 있다. 사실 개의 시력은 움직임에 아주 민감하다. 가장 작은 자세의 변화조차도 개에게는 큰 의미가 있다. 이는 개를 훈련할 때 명심해야 할 중요한 것이다. 말로 명령하지 않고도 개가 움직이도록 하고 싶다면, 개가 이해할 수 있게 항상 같은 몸짓을 사용해야 한다.

어휘 based on …에 근거하여 solely[sóulli] 男 오직 appearance[əpíərəns] 명 외모, 모습 motionless[móuʃənlis] 형 움직임이 없는 gesture[dʒéstʃər] 명 제스처, 몸짓 in addition to … 외에도 posture[pástʃər] 명 자세 keep in mind 명심하다 train[trein] 동 훈련하다 command[kəmǽnd] 명 명령 [문제] dull[dʌl] 형 지루한; *둔한

구문 9행 This is important to keep in mind [**when training** your dog].
- when training 이하는 때를 나타내는 분사구문으로, 의미를 명확하게 하기 위해 접속사를 생략하지 않음

10행 …, you must always use the same gestures to **allow** your dog **to understand**.
- allow + 목적어 + to-v: …가 ~하게 하다

VOCABULARY REVIEW

A **1** vision **2** surface **3** directly **4** depth
B **1** tell **2** commands **3** sensitive **4** surroundings **5** motionless   C **1** d **2** a

★*Give Me a Hug!*

1 c **2** c **3** b **4** It leads to decreased blood pressure, less stress, and a lower risk of heart disease. **5** b **6** c

> 몇 년 전, 한 남자가 시드니의 가장 붐비는 거리에서 모르는 사람들에게 프리 허그를 해주며 서 있었다. 누군가 이것을 동영상으로 만들어 온라인에 올렸고, 그것은 곧 전 세계적인 선풍을 일으켰다. 이 동영상을 볼 기회가 생긴다면, 한 가지가 정말 눈에 띌 것인데, 바로 포옹을 하는 사람들이 모두 크게 미소를 짓는다는 것이다. 포옹은 우리의 기분을 더 좋게 해주는데, 이제 과학자들이 그 이유를 증명했다.
>
> 한 가지 이유는 포옹이 실제로 감정에 직접적인 영향을 준다는 것이다. 우선, 포옹이라는 행위가 도파민과 같이 기분을 좋게 하는 화학 물질을 뇌에 분비시킨다. 게다가 노스캐롤라이나 대학의 Karen Grewen 박사가 주도한 연구에서 포옹은 신체가 옥시토신을 더 많이 만들어내도록 한다는 것이 밝혀졌다. <u>그것은 배려와 유대감과 관련된 화학 물질이다.</u> 그래서 더 높은 옥시토신 수치는 우리가 다른 사람에게 더 다정하게 대하도록 한다. 아마도 이것이 연인들이 포옹을 그렇게 많이 즐기는 이유일 것이다.
>
> 우리의 감정과 관련된 화학 물질을 활성화하는 것 외에도 포옹은 우리의 몸에 좋다. 더 높은 옥시토신 수치는 신체적 건강, 특히 심장과도 연관되어 있다. 예를 들어 Grewen이 주도한 다른 연구에서, 포옹이 혈압을 낮추고, 스트레스를 줄이며, 심장 질환의 위험을 낮춘다는 것이 밝혀졌다.
>
> 이 연구는 사람들이 지금보다 더 자주 포옹을 해야 한다고 제안한다. 포옹은 배우자나 어린아이들만을 위해서 남겨두어서는 안 된다. 대신, 사람들은 친구와 가족들, 심지어 직장 동료나 이웃들과도 더 기꺼이 포옹해야 한다. 그렇게 하면 모두가 포옹의 정신적, 신체적 혜택을 누릴 수 있다!

어휘 hug[hʌg] 똉 포옹 똉 포옹하다   sensation[senséiʃən] 똉 느낌; *선풍, 돌풍   clip[klip]
똉 핀, 클립; *(영화 등의) 클립(일부만 따로 떼어서 보여 주는 부분)   stand out 두드러지다
impact[ímpækt] 똉 영향   pleasurable[pléʒərəbl] 똉 즐거운   chemical[kémikəl] 똉 화학 물질
dopamine[dóupəmìːn] 똉 도파민   oxytocin[àksitóusn] 똉 옥시토신   activate[ǽktəvèit]
똉 작동시키다, 활성화하다   be concerned with …와 관계가 있다   lead to (결과적으로) …에 이르다,
…하게 되다   save[seiv] 똉 남겨두다   be willing to-v 기꺼이 …하다   workmate[wə́ːrkmèit]
똉 (직장) 동료   mental[méntl] 똉 정신적인   [문제] be associated with …와 연관이 있다
caring[kɛ́əriŋ] 똉 상냥함, 친절함   bonding[bándiŋ] 똉 유대

구문 1행 …, a man stood in the busiest street in Sydney [**offering** free hugs to strangers].
　　　　• offering 이하는 동시동작을 나타내는 분사구문
　　8행 In addition, a study [**led** by Dr. Karen … North Carolina] found that hugging
　　　　causes the body *to produce* more oxytocin.
　　　　• led 이하는 a study를 수식하는 과거분사구
　　　　• cause + 목적어 + to-v: …가 ∼하게 하다
　　11행 Perhaps this is (the reason) **why** couples enjoy hugging so much.
　　　　• why: 이유를 나타내는 관계부사로, 앞에 선행사 the reason이 생략되어 있음
　　18행 This research **suggests** that people **should hug** more often than they *do* ….
　　　　• 제안을 나타내는 동사 suggest 뒤에 이어지는 that절의 동사는 'should + 동사원형'을 쓰는데,
　　　　　should는 종종 생략됨
　　　　• do: 반복되는 부분인 hug를 대신하는 대동사

STRATEGIC SUMMARY   released, increases, care, health, recommend

1 d **2** 1) F 2) T

> 요즈음, Juan Mann 덕택에 프리 허그를 발견하는 것이 쉽다. 여기 그의 이야기가 있다.
>
> 나는 도착 터미널에 서서 다른 사람들 모두가 웃고 친구와 가족들과 포옹하는 것을 보았다. 나는 정말로 누군가가 나를 안아주기를 원했다. 그래서 나는 '프리 허그'라고 쓰여 있는 종이 표지판을 만들어서 도시의 가장 붐비는 길모퉁이로 가져갔다. 처음에는 아무도 날 거들떠보지도 않았다. 그런데, 그때 한 여성이 다가와서 자신의 개가 그날 아침에 막 죽었고 딸은 정확히 일 년 전에 죽었다고 말했다. 그래서 나는 한쪽 무릎을 꿇고, 그녀에게 팔을 둘러 포옹을 해주었다. 우리가 떨어진 후, 그 여자는 미소를 짓고 있었다.

어휘   thanks to …의 덕택으로   arrival[əráivəl] 몡 도착   notice[nóutis] 동 알아차리다
cardboard[káːrdbɔ̀ːrd] 몡 판지   sign[sain] 몡 표지판   get down …을 굽히다, 구부리다
part[paːrt] 동 헤어지다; *갈라지다   [문제] comfort[kʌ́mfərt] 동 위로하다   respond to …에 응하다

구문   3행   … I **noticed** all the other people **laughing** and **hugging** their friends ….
· 지각동사(notice) + 목적어 + v-ing: …가 ~하는 것을 알아차리다
8행   … said her dog just died that morning and that her daughter **had died** exactly one year before.
· had died: 주절의 시제보다 앞선 시점의 내용을 가리키는 과거완료

VOCABULARY REVIEW

A **1** part **2** risk **3** sensation **4** bonding
B **1** suggest **2** got down **3** particularly **4** saving **5** mental   **C** **1** c **2** b

unit 15 FASHION

pp. 64-67

*Full Figured Fashion Week

1 d **2** They are larger, more realistic-looking models. **3** c **4** b **5** d **6** 1) T 2) F

> 패션계에서 일어나는 일들의 경향을 따라가기를 좋아하는가? 그렇다면 올해의 큰 사이즈를 위한 패션 위크에 참가해야 한다. 수십 년간, 패션 산업은 사이즈가 더 큰, 더 현실적인 모습의 모델들을 무시해 왔다. 대신, 가장 유명한 패션은 건강하지 않게 깡마른 모델들이 입는다. 일부 모델들은 마른 상태를 유지하려 애쓰다가 식이 장애로 사망하기까지 했다. FFFWeek는 패션계에서 책임감의 복귀를 목표로 한다.
>
> FFFWeek는 전직 큰 사이즈 모델이었던 Gwendolyn DeVoe에 의해 설립되었다. 그녀와 그녀의 동료들은 매년 뉴욕, 런던, 밀라노, 파리에서 열리는 전통적인 패션 위크 행사에서 간과되는 것이 지켜웠다. 그래서 2009년 DeVoe는 FFFWeek를 설립했다. 그녀의 의도 중 하나는 큰 사이즈의 의상 디자인과 그 의상을 입는 모델들을 위한 지지를 장려하는 것이었다. 그녀는 또한 전통적인 패션 모델 일의 건강상 위험에 대한 관심을 끌어들이기 원했다. 패션업에서 일하는 모델만이 위험에 처한 것은 아니다. 또한, 전 세계의 여성들은 깡마른 모델들에 의해 정립된 비현실적인 미의 기준을 본다. 그들 스스로가 그 기준에 이르지 못할 때, 여성들은 정신적 그리고 신체적으로 모두 고통을 받는다.
>
> FFFWeek는 뉴욕 시에서 6월에 열린다. 패션쇼 이외에 그룹 토론과 디자이너 경연 대회도 있다. 세계 최대의 패션 회사 대표들을 포함하여 천 명이 넘는 사람들이 매년 FFFWeek에 참가한다. 시간이 흐르면 FFFWeek는 반드시 성장할 것이고, 그럼에 따라 그것은 패션과 건강의 관계에 관한 진실을 계속해서 사람들에게 가르칠 것이다.

어휘   keep current with …의 동향을 알다   full figured (여성이) 체격이 큰; *(옷 등이) 큰 사이즈의

decade[dékeid] 圈 10년　realistic[rìːəlístik] 圈 현실적인　skinny[skíni] 圈 깡마른　die from
…로 죽다　eating disorder 식이 장애　aim for …을 목표로 하다　responsibility[rispὰnsəbíləti]
圈 책임감　former[fɔ́ːrmər] 圈 이전의　plus-size[plʌ́ssaiz] 圈 체격이 큰, 큰 사이즈의
colleague[káliːg] 圈 동료　be tired of …가 지겹다　overlook[òuvərlúk] 圈 간과하다
intention[inténʃən] 圈 의도　draw attention to …에 관심을 끌어들이다　hazard[hǽzərd]
圈 위험　at risk 위험에 처한　representative[rèprizéntətiv] 圈 대표자　with time
시간이 흐름에 따라　[문제] trendy[tréndi] 圈 최신 유행의　disregard[dìsrigάːrd] 圈 무시하다
unavoidable[ὰnəvɔ́idəbl] 圈 불가피한　outfit[áutfit] 圈 옷

구문　1행　Do you like to keep current with **what**'s going on in the fashion world?
　　　• what: '…하는 것'의 의미로, 선행사를 포함하는 관계대명사(= the thing which)

4행　... are worn by models [**who** are unhealthily skinny].
　　　• who 이하는 models를 수식하는 주격 관계대명사절

9행　She and her colleagues were tired of [**being** overlooked] at the traditional
Fashion Week events [*held* in New York, …].
　　　• being 이하는 전치사 of의 목적어 역할을 하는 동명사구
　　　• held 이하는 the traditional Fashion Week events를 수식하는 과거분사구

STRATEGIC ORGANIZER　plus-size, awareness, realistic, contest, Attended

EXPANDING KNOWLEDGE

1 d　**2** d

패션 산업에 따르면, 아름다운 것은 극히 마른 것이다. 그것이 많은 사람들이 모델의 외양을 규제함으로써 보다 건강한
이상형을 장려하라고 패션 산업에 요청해 온 이유이다. '0사이즈 논쟁'은 세 명의 모델이 지나치게 마른 것으로 인한
건강 문제로 사망한 이후 관심을 끌었다. 대부분의 모델들은 0사이즈이고, 그들의 체질량 지수는 16 혹은 그 이하인데,
이는 그들을 기아의 위험에 처하게 한다. 이에 응하여, 마드리드는 체질량 지수 18 미만의 모델을 금지하기 시작했다.
밀라노와 미국은 곧 (이를) 따랐다. 그럼에도 불구하고, 이 금지안이 효과적이기 위해서는 디자이너들과 소비자들은 더
많은 것을 해야 한다. 디자이너는 패션쇼 무대에 깡마른 모델을 쓰지 말아야 한다. 그리고 소비자들은 비현실적으로
마른 모델을 광고에 쓰는 브랜드에 대해 불매 운동을 해야 한다.

어휘　promote[prəmóut] 圈 장려하다, 촉진하다　ideal[aidíːəl] 圈 이상형 圈 이상적인　regulate[régjulèit]
圈 규제하다　due to … 때문에　starvation[staːrvéiʃən] 圈 기아　ban[bæn] 圈 금지하다 圈 금지(법)
runway[rʌ́nwèi] 圈 패션쇼 무대　boycott[bɔ́ikat] 圈 불매 운동하다　[문제] expel[ikspél]
圈 내쫓다, 쫓아버리다　take action 조치를 취하다

구문　1행　**To be** beautiful is **to be** extremely skinny, according to the fashion industry.
　　　• To be와 to be는 각각 주어와 보어로 쓰인 명사적 용법의 to부정사

2행　That's (the reason) **why** many have *called for* the industry *to promote* ....
　　　• why: 이유를 나타내는 관계부사로, 앞에 선행사 the reason이 생략되어 있음
　　　• call for ... to-v: …에게 ～하는 것을 요청하다

4행　... since three models died due to health problems from [**being** too thin].
　　　• being 이하는 전치사 from의 목적어 역할을 하는 동명사구

VOCABULARY REVIEW

A　**1** former　**2** hazard　**3** promote　**4** starvation
B　**1** intention　**2** due to　**3** overlooked　**4** at risk　**5** boycotted　　　**C**　**1** c　**2** c

★*The Mother Teresa Effect*

1 c **2** b **3** c **4** They can experience a feeling of happiness and energy followed by a "helper's high" of peace and calm. **5** a **6** 1) F 2) T

당신이 마지막으로 다른 사람을 도운 것은 언제인가? 아마도 당신은 노인이 계단을 오르는 것을 돕거나 자선 단체에 기부를 했을지도 모른다. 이런 친절 행동이 당신의 기분을 어떻게 만들었는지 기억하는가? 연구는 다른 사람들을 돕는 것이 우리의 기분을 더 좋게 만들 수 있고 심지어 신체 건강도 증진할 수 있다는 것을 시사한다. 이 현상은 테레사 수녀 효과라고 알려져 있다.

그 용어는 하버드 대학에서 실시된 한 실험에서 유래했다. 연구원들은 132명의 학생들에게 20세기 인도 캘커타의 가난하고 아픈 사람들을 도왔던 천주교 수녀인 테레사 수녀의 업적에 대한 영화를 보여 주었다. (테레사 수녀는 행복은 기도 없이는 찾을 수 없다고 말했다.) 그 영화가 끝나고, 연구원들은 학생들의 면역 글로불린 항체 A 수치를 측정했는데, 그것은 바이러스에 대한 신체의 첫 방어 물질 중 하나이다. 놀랍게도, 그들의 면역 글로불린 항체 A 수치는 단순히 테레사 수녀가 자선 활동을 하는 것을 지켜본 후에 상당히 증가했다.

그러면 누군가 자선 행위를 하는 것을 보는 것이 사람들에게 그토록 강한 영향을 미친다면, 실제로 직접 자선 행위를 하는 것의 효과는 어떠할까? Allan Luks와 Penny Payne이 실시한 3,000명의 자원봉사자에 대한 한 연구는 다양한 심리적, 신체적 이점을 발견했다. 그 자원봉사자들은 평화와 평온의 '다른 이를 도울 때 느끼는 만족감'을 수반하는 행복감과 활력을 경험했다. 신체적으로, 자원봉사자들은 자원봉사 후에 스트레스, 만성 통증, 그리고 불면증과 같은 일부 건강 문제가 감소된 것을 발견했다.

이 모든 증거는 다른 사람들을 돕는 것이 우리의 마음뿐만 아니라 건강에도 긍정적인 영향을 끼친다는 것을 보여 준다. 다른 사람들을 돕는 것은 또한 우리 자신을 돕는 것을 의미하니, 이를 시도해보는 것이 어떤가?

어휘 donation[dounéiʃən] 몡 기부, 기증   charity[tʃǽrəti] 몡 자선 단체; 자선   originate[ərídʒənèit] 통 유래하다   conduct[kəndʌ́kt] 통 수행하다   nun[nʌn] 몡 수녀   measure[méʒər] 통 측정하다, 재다   immunoglobulin[ìmjunouglábjulin] 몡 면역 글로불린 항체   defense[diféns] 몡 방어; *방어물   significantly[signífikəntli] 閈 상당히, 크게   volunteer[vàləntíər] 몡 자원봉사자 통 자원봉사를 하다   helper's high 다른 이를 도울 때 느끼는 만족감   calm[kaːm] 몡 고요, 평온   chronic[kránik] 휑 만성적인   insomnia[insámniə] 몡 불면증   evidence[évədəns] 몡 증거   give it a try 시도하다, 한번 해보다   [문제] dedicate[dédikèit] 통 헌신하다   immune system 면역 체계   worsen[wə́ːrsn] 통 악화시키다

구문   3행   Do you remember [**how** this act of kindness made you feel]?
　　　　　• how 이하는 '의문사 + 주어 + 동사' 어순의 간접의문문으로, 동사 remember의 목적어 역할을 함
　　　　9행   The term originated from a study [**conducted** at Harvard University].
　　　　　• conducted 이하는 a study를 수식하는 과거분사구
　　　　14행   … immunoglobulin A, **which** is one of the body's first defenses against viruses.
　　　　　• which: immunoglobulin A를 보충 설명하는 계속적 용법의 주격 관계대명사
　　　　18행   So, if [**watching** someone *performing* acts of charity] **has** such **a** strong **effect on** people, …?
　　　　　• watching 이하는 if절의 주어로 쓰인 동명사구
　　　　　• 지각동사(watch) + 목적어 + v-ing: …가 ~하고 있는 것을 보다
　　　　　• have an effect on: …에 영향을 미치다

STRATEGIC ORGANIZER   helping, increase, charity, happiness, health

EXPANDING KNOWLEDGE

1 d　**2** 1) T　2) F

테레사 수녀는 알바니아에서 태어났다. 열여덟 살에, 그녀는 수도회에 들어가 수녀가 되었다. 몇 년 후, 그녀는 인도로 이주했고 가난한 사람들의 복지에 일생을 바치기로 결심했다. 1950년 10월 7일, 테레사 수녀는 가난하고 병들고 고아가 된 사람들을 돕기 위해 사랑의 선교수녀회를 시작했다. 그것은 전국의 많은 지역에 퍼져 있는 지사를 갖추어 그녀의 모든 활동의 중심지가 되었다. 오늘날, 사랑의 선교수녀회는 아시아, 아프리카, 동유럽, 그리고 라틴 아메리카의 여러 국가에 있는 가난한 사람들을 돕는다. 이들 지역에서, 그 단체는 자연재해 구호물자를 제공하고, 알코올 중독자, 노숙자, 그리고 에이즈 환자를 돌본다.

어휘　religious order 수도회　welfare[wélfɛər] 명 복지, 행복　missionary[míʃənèri] 명 선교사
orphan[ɔ́ːrfən] 통 고아로 만들다　branch[bræntʃ] 명 나뭇가지; *지사　relief[rilíːf] 명 안도; *구호, 구호물자　disaster[dizǽstər] 명 재난, 재해　alcoholic[ælkəhɔ́ːlik] 명 알코올 중독자
homeless[hóumlis] 형 집이 없는　sufferer[sʌ́fərər] 명 고통받는 사람, 환자
[문제] establish[istǽbliʃ] 통 설립하다

구문　4행　... the Missionaries of Charity **to help** the poor, sick, and orphaned.
　　　　• to help: '…하기 위해'라는 의미로, 목적을 나타내는 부사적 용법의 to부정사
　　　　• the + 형용사[분사]: '…한 사람들'이라는 의미의 복수 보통 명사
　　　5행　... the center of all her activities **with** its branches **spread** to many parts ....
　　　　• with + 명사 + v-ed: '…가 ~된 채로'라는 의미의 분사구문으로, 명사와 분사가 수동 관계일 때 과거분사를 씀

VOCABULARY REVIEW

A　*1* welfare　*2* dedicate　*3* chronic　*4* relief
B　*1* disaster　*2* donation　*3* volunteers　*4* branch　*5* measure　　**C**　*1* c　*2* b

unit
17 SPACE

pp. 72-75

★The Moon

1 b　**2** The moon's gravitational pull on Earth's oceans slows its rotation.　**3** b　**4** d　**5** c　**6** d

사람들은 맑은 날 밤에 달을 바라보는 것을 즐긴다. 달은 예술에 영감을 주었고, 신화를 만들었으며, 언어에 영향을 미쳤다. 게다가 달의 움직임은 지구를 살기 적합한 곳으로 만드는 데 필수적인 역할을 한다. 그런데 달이 존재하지 않으면 삶은 어떻게 될까?

분명히, 달이 없다면 월식이나 일식은 발생하지 않을 것이다. 하지만 이것은 시작에 불과하다. 지구의 해수에 미치는 달의 인력이 지구의 자전을 늦추기 때문에, 달이 없다면 우리 행성은 훨씬 더 빨리 회전하게 될 것이다. 수십억 년 전, 달의 형성 이전에 하루의 길이는 10시간에 불과했다. 달이 없다면 하루는 여전히 이렇게 짧을 것이다.

지구가 이렇게 빨리 자전하면, 바람이 훨씬 더 세질 것이다. 거대 가스 행성인 목성을 생각해보면, 그것은 지구보다 훨씬 더 빨리 회전한다. <u>목성의 폭풍은 거대하고 지구의 폭풍보다 몇 배가 더 크다.</u> 그리고 그것들은 몇 세기 동안 지속되고 행성 전체로 퍼진다. 이 강한 폭풍이 목성이 띠를 두른 모습을 갖게 하는 것이다. 달이 존재하지 않는다면, 지구도 비슷한 날씨를 갖게 될지도 모른다.

지구의 바람이 이렇게 강해지면 삶이 제한될 것이다. 지속적으로 바람이 휘몰아치는데 거리를 걷거나 친구와 이야기 나누는 모습을 상상해보라. 항공과 해상 여행이 거의 불가능해지고, 이는 생각과 기술의 교류를 저해할 것이다. 심지어 일부 생명체들은 존재할 수조차 없게 될 것이다!

우주에서 우리와 가장 가까운 이웃은 우리의 행성을 형성하는 데 중요한 역할을 해왔다. 그러므로 다음에 달을 볼 때는, 그것이 해온 역할과 그것이 없다면 우리의 행성이 어떻게 달라질지 생각해보라!

어휘 gaze[ɡeiz] 통 바라보다, 응시하다   moon[muːn] 명 달; 위성   shape[ʃeip] (중요한 영향을 미쳐) 형성하다   mythology[miθálədʒi] 명 신화   habitable[hǽbitəbl] 형 살 수 있는, 거주할 만한   obviously[ábviəsli] 부 분명히   lunar[lúːnər] 형 달의   solar[sóulər] 형 태양의   eclipse[iklíps] 명 (일식·월식의) 식   rotation[routéiʃən] 명 회전, 자전 (rotate 통 회전하다)   billion[bíljən] 명 10억   stretch[stretʃ] 통 퍼지다, 뻗어 나가다   banded[bǽndid] 형 줄무늬 모양의, 띠의   constantly[kánstəntli] 부 지속적으로   howling[háuliŋ] 형 휘몰아치는   exchange[ikstʃéindʒ] 명 교환   probable[prábəbl] 형 (어떤 일이) 있음 직한   [문제] windstorm[wíndstɔːrm] 명 폭풍   enormous[inɔ́ːrməs] 형 거대한   enhance[inhǽns] 통 향상시키다   restrict[ristríkt] 통 제한하다   accelerate[æksélərèit] 통 가속화하다

구문 3행 So what **would** life **be** like **if** the moon **didn't exist**?
· if + 주어 + 동사의 과거형, 주어 + 조동사의 과거형 + 동사원형: 가정법 과거

6행 **Without** the moon, our planet **would spin** *much* faster because ....
· '…가 없다면 ~할 텐데'의 의미의 가정법 과거 문장으로, without이 이끄는 구가 if절을 대신함
· much: '훨씬'의 의미로, 비교급을 강조하는 부사

12행 Its windstorms are enormous — **many times larger than** those on Earth.
· 배수사 + 비교급 + than: …보다 ~배 더 …한

24행 ..., think of the role [(which[that]) **it has played**] and [*how* different our planet would be without it]!
· it has played 앞에 the role을 선행사로 하는 목적격 관계대명사가 생략되어 있음
· how 이하는 '의문사 + 주어 + 동사' 어순의 간접의문문으로, the role과 함께 think of의 목적어 역할을 함

STRATEGIC ORGANIZER eclipses, shorter, similar, extinct

EXPANDING KNOWLEDGE

1 d **2** c

사람들은 수천 년 동안 달을 봐왔다. 달의 지속적인 존재는 달을 세계의 모든 문화에서 이야기와 전설의 소재로 만들었다. 예를 들어, 남아프리카 부시먼은 월식을 어둠 속에서 사냥을 할 수 있도록 발로 달을 감싸고 있는 사자의 이야기로 설명한다. 많은 문화에서 달은 흔히 변화와 죽음, 부활의 상징으로 기능했다. 달과 관련된 많은 미신들도 있다. 중세 유럽에서는 달빛 아래에서 잠을 자는 것이 사람을 미치게 만든다고 여겨졌는데, 이것이 달을 의미하는 라틴어에 바탕을 둔 '미치광이(lunatic)'라는 단어의 기원이다. 물론 우리는 모두 보름달일 때 늑대 인간으로 변하는 사람들에 대해 들어본 적이 있다. 분명히, 달은 사람들의 문화적 배경에 관계없이 그들의 상상력의 중심부를 차지하고 있다.

어휘 continuous[kəntínjuəs] 형 지속적인   presence[prézns] 명 존재   paw[pɔː] 명 (동물의) 발   rebirth[riːbə́ːrθ] 명 부활   plenty of 많은   superstition[sùːpərstíʃən] 명 미신   medieval[mìːdiíːvəl] 형 중세의   lunatic[lúːnətik] 명 미치광이 형 미친   transform[trænsfɔ́ːrm] 통 변신하다   werewolf[wɛ́ərwulf] 명 늑대 인간   occupy[ákjupài] 통 점유하다, 차지하다   central[séntrəl] 형 중심의   background[bǽkgràund] 명 배경   [문제] along with …와 함께   regardless of …와 무관하게   according to …에 의하면

구문 9행 ..., [**sleeping** under the moonlight] was thought to *drive* people *mad*; ....

- sleeping 이하는 문장의 주어로 쓰인 동명사구
- drive + 목적어 + mad: …을 미치게 하다

VOCABULARY REVIEW

A **1** probable **2** habitable **3** rotate **4** transform
B **1** presence **2** spins **3** gazed at **4** legends **5** medieval   C **1** b **2** c

unit *18* MYSTERIES

pp. 76-79

Piri's Map

1 a **2** Because it was one of the oldest maps to show America. **3** b **4** d **5** a, b **6** *1)* F *2)* T

> 1929년, 터키에서 연구하던 사학자들은 오래된 지도를 한 장 발견했다. 그것은 1513년에 Piri라는 이름의 터키 해군 제독에 의해 만들어졌다. 이 지도는 미국을 보여주는 가장 오래된 지도 중 하나였기 때문에 사람들의 관심을 끌었다. 하지만 이 지도에는 오늘날 대부분의 지도가 사용하는 위선과 경선이 없기 때문에, 사람들은 그것이 부정확하다고 생각했다.
>
> 그러나 이 생각은 1953년에 바뀌었다. 한 연구자는 그 지도가 위치를 보여주기 위해 많은 원형의 점을 사용하는 것을 발견했다. 그 지도를 격자 눈금과 지구본 위에 옮겨 놓았을 때, 그는 그것이 아주 정확하다는 것을 발견했다. 사실, 그 지도는 아주 정확해서 미 공군은 그것을 이용해 자신들의 지도에 있는 실수를 바로잡았다. (곧 그들은 자신들의 실수를 인정하고 Piri의 지도를 사용하는 것을 그만두었다.)
>
> 또 다른 놀라운 사실은 그 지도가 남극대륙을 포함하고 있다는 것이다. 남극대륙은 그 지도가 만들어지고 300년이 지난 후인 1820년이 되어서야 발견되었다. 하지만 훨씬 더 엄청난 미스터리는 그것이 남극대륙의 해안선을 정확하게 보여주고 있다는 것이다. 전문가들의 말에 따르면, 남극대륙은 6천 년 넘게 얼음으로 덮여 있었다. 그렇다면 Piri는 어떻게 얼음 밑에 있는 땅을 그릴 수 있었을까?
>
> 사실, Piri는 그의 지도를 그리기 위해 다른 많은 고대 지도들을 참고했다. 어떤 사람들은 고대 문명이 남극대륙이 얼음으로 덮이기 전에 그것을 발견했고 지도로 그렸다고 믿는다. 그 정확도에 대해서, 다른 사람들은 심지어 Piri가 우주에서 온 외계인들의 도움을 받았다고 주장한다. 하지만 우리가 증거를 더 찾을 때까지, Piri의 지도는 계속 미스터리로 남아 있을 것 같다.

어휘 historian[histɔ́ːriən] 명 사학자   map[mæp] 명 지도 동 지도를 만들다[그리다]   admiral[ǽdmərəl] 명 해군 장성, 제독   inaccurate[inǽkjərit] 명 부정확한 (accurate 형 정확한 accurately 부 정확하게 accuracy 명 정확도)   circular[sə́ːrkjulər] 형 원형의, 둥근   transfer[trænsfə́r] 동 옮기다, 이동하다   grid[grid] 명 격자무늬; *(지도의) 격자 눈금   globe[gloub] 명 지구본   correct[kərékt] 동 바로잡다, 정정하다   Antarctica[æntɑ́ːrktikə] 명 남극대륙 (antarctic 형 남극의)   coastline[kóustlàin] 명 해안선   consult[kənsʌ́lt] 동 상담하다; *참고하다   civilization[sìvəlizéiʃən] 명 문명   as to …에 관해서는   alien[éiljən] 명 외계인   outer space 우주 공간   [문제] existence[igzístəns] 명 존재

구문
1행　In 1929, historians [**working** in Turkey] found an old map.
　　• working 이하는 historians를 수식하는 현재분사구

3행　... because it was one of the oldest maps **to show** America.
　　• to show: one of the oldest maps를 수식하는 형용사적 용법의 to부정사

4행　However, because the map does not have the lines of latitude and longitude [**that** most maps use today], ...

• that 이하는 the lines of latitude and longitude를 수식하는 목적격 관계대명사절

14행 Antarctica was **not** discovered **until** 1820, 300 years after the map was made.
• not … until ~: ~해서야 비로소 …하다

16행 But an **even** greater mystery is that ….
• even: '훨씬'의 의미로, 비교급을 강조하는 부사

STRATEGIC ORGANIZER   drawn, Accurate, coastline, civilizations, Creatures

EXPANDING KNOWLEDGE

1 d   **2** 1) F 2) F

> Piri Reis는 터키의 Gallipoli에서 1465년에서 1470년 사이에 태어났다. 그는 어린 나이에 오스만 제국의 해군에 입대해서, 바다에서 전투를 하며 수년을 보냈다. 그는 1511년에 Gallipoli로 귀향하여 그가 배운 것들을 적기 시작했다. 1513년에, 그는 놀랄 만큼 정확한 세계 지도를 만들어냈다. 그러고 나서, 1521년에 그는 *항해의 책*을 쓰는 것을 끝냈다. 그 책은 290개의 지도를 담고 있었고 나침반을 사용하는 기술과 별을 이용하여 방향을 찾는 방법을 포함한 많은 정보를 제공했다. 이러한 중요한 기여에도 불구하고, 그는 다시 전쟁에 나가기를 거부했다는 이유로 90세 즈음에 처형되었다.

어휘   navy[néivi] 명 해군   empire[émpaiər] 명 제국   navigation[nævəɡéiʃən] 명 항해(술)
technique[tekníːk] 명 기법, 기술   compass[kʌ́mpəs] 명 나침반   direction[dirékʃən] 명 방향
contribution[kàntrəbjúːʃən] 명 기부금; *기여, 이바지   execute[éksikjùːt] 동 처형하다
refuse[rifjúːz] 동 거절[거부]하다   [문제] unjust[ʌ̀ndʒʌ́st] 형 불공평한, 부당한
biography[baiáɡrəfi] 명 전기, 일대기   achievement[ətʃíːvmənt] 명 업적

구문   3행   …, and **spent many years fighting** at sea.
• spend + 시간 + v-ing: …하는 데 (시간)을 보내다

8행   … the technique of **using** a compass and methods of **finding** directions using the stars.
• using과 finding은 각각 앞의 전치사 of의 목적어 역할을 하는 동명사

VOCABULARY REVIEW

A   **1** admiral   **2** alien   **3** globe   **4** compass
B   **1** correct   **2** executed   **3** admit   **4** expert   **5** contribution   C   **1** a   **2** b

unit
19 ART   pp. 80-83

★*Claude Monet*

1 a   **2** It is more abstract, and the vibrant colors are gone.   **3** b   **4** a   **5** d   **6** 1) T 2) F

> 1912년, 72세의 나이에, 위대한 프랑스 인상주의 화가 클로드 모네는 백내장에 걸렸다는 사실을 알게 되었다. "나는 더 이상 같은 명암으로 색을 볼 수 없었어."라고 한번은 그가 친구에게 말했다. "빨간색이 내게는 어둡게 보이고, 분홍색은 따분하고, 혼합된 색과 낮은 톤은 아예 눈에 띄지 않게 되어버렸어."
> 　모네의 후기 작품은 초기 작품들과 화법에 있어서 많이 다르다. 그것들은 보다 추상적이며, 강렬한 색은 사라졌다. 왜 이런 일이 생겼던 것일까? 안과 의사이자 예술 애호가인 Michael Marmor에게 이론이 하나 있다. 그는 모네의 시력이 대부분의 색을 노란색과 갈색의 색조로 보이게 했다고 주장한다. 이를 바탕으로 Marmor 교수는 모네 그림을

그가 봤을 법한 대로 재현했다. 그의 작품들은 모네의 그림을 흐릿하고 칙칙하게 보여준다. 이것이 정말로 모네가 그의 작품을 보았던 방식이라면, 그것은 나이가 들면서 그가 파란색을 더 많이 사용했던 이유를 설명할지도 모른다. 즉 노랗게 된 시야를 보완하기 위해서였을 것이다.

Marmor 교수의 작업에도 불구하고, 모든 미술학자들이 모네가 자신의 상태 때문에 화법을 바꿨다고 확신하지는 않는다. 한 비평가는 백내장을 제거하는 수술 전후의 모네의 그림이 비슷해 보인다고 주장한다. 다른 사람들은 모네는 뛰어난 화가였고 그의 화법에서의 어떤 변화든지 의도적이었을 것이라고 주장한다. 비록 모네 작품에서의 변화를 설명해 보고자 하는 많은 가설이 있지만, 우리가 확실히 아는 것은 모네가 직면한 어려움에도 불구하고, 그의 예술은 계속해서 영감을 준다는 점이다.

어휘 Impressionist[impréʃənist] 몡 인상파 화가　intensity[inténsəti] 몡 강도; *명암　tone[toun] 몡 어조; *색조　escape[iskéip] 통 탈출하다; *눈에 띄지 않다　abstract[æbstrækt] 혱 추상적인　vibrant[váibrənt] 혱 강렬한, 선명한　theory[θíːəri] 몡 이론　recreate[rìːkriéit] 통 재현하다　blurry[blə́ːri] 혱 흐릿한　dull[dʌl] 혱 따분한; *칙칙한　compensate[kámpənsèit] 통 보상하다; *보완하다　convinced[kənvínst] 혱 확신하는　surgery[sə́ːrdʒəri] 몡 수술　intentional[inténʃənl] 혱 의도적인 (intend 통 의도하다)　hypothesis[haipάθəsis] 몡 가설 (pl. hypotheses)　attempt[ətémpt] 통 시도하다　[문제] overcome[òuvərkʌ́m] 통 극복하다　hardship[háːrdʃip] 몡 고난　have difficulty v-ing …하는 데 어려움을 겪다　confess[kənfés] 통 고백하다　treatment[tríːtmənt] 몡 치료

구문
10행　… recreated Monet's paintings as he probably **would have seen** them.
　　• would have v-ed: 가정법 과거완료
12행　If this is **how**[the way] Monet really saw his work, it may explain (the reason) *why* he used more blues ….
　　• how: 방법을 나타내는 관계부사로, 선행사 the way와 함께 쓰지 않음
　　• why: 이유를 나타내는 관계부사로, 앞에 선행사 the reason이 생략되어 있음
15행　…, **not all** art scholars are convinced that Monet changed his style ….
　　• not all: '모두 …인 것은 아니다'라는 의미의 부분부정
21행　…, **what** we know for sure is [*that* Monet's art continues to inspire, despite the difficulties (which[that]) **he faced**].
　　• what: '…하는 것'의 의미로 선행사를 포함하는 관계대명사(= the thing which)
　　• that: 동사 is의 보어 역할을 하는 명사절을 이끄는 접속사
　　• he faced 앞에 the difficulties를 선행사로 하는 목적격 관계대명사가 생략되어 있음

STRATEGIC SUMMARY　vision, differently, lacks, disagree, intentional

EXPANDING KNOWLEDGE

1 d　**2** The light, the color, and the energetic qualities of nature were emphasized.

인상주의는 한 회화 양식에 주어진 이름인데, 그 이름은 어디에서 온 것일까? 1872년에 프랑스 화가 클로드 모네는 *인상, 해돋이*라는 제목의 그림을 그렸는데, 그것은 수면에서 춤추는 햇빛을 보여준다. 그 이후로 계속, 모네는 그의 화법을 가리키기 위해 인상주의라는 이름을 사용했다. 빛과 색, 활기 넘치는 자연의 특성이 인상주의 운동에 의해 강조되었다. 드가와 피사로 같은 화가들은 이러한 찰나적이고 기쁨을 주는 자연적 아름다움의 순간들을 자신들의 그림에 담는 데 모네와 함께했다. 그들이 만든 그 운동은 1870년부터 1910년까지 지속되었고 오늘날도 여전히 느낄 수 있는 방식으로 미술계에 영향을 끼쳤다.

어휘 Impressionism[impréʃənìzm] 몡 인상주의　surface[sə́ːrfis] 몡 표면　energetic[ènərdʒétik] 혱 활기가 넘치는　emphasize[émfəsàiz] 통 강조하다　capture[kǽptʃər] 통 (필름·화폭 등에) 담다　fleeting[flíːtiŋ] 혱 순식간의, 잠깐 동안의　joyous[dʒɔ́iəs] 혱 기쁨을 주는　last[læst] 통 지속되다

구문 3행 ... a painting [**titled** *Impression, Sunrise*], *which* shows sunlight dancing on the surface of water.
- titled 이하는 a painting을 수식하는 과거분사구
- which: *Impression, Sunrise*를 보충 설명하는 계속적 용법의 주격 관계대명사

VOCABULARY REVIEW

A **1** blurry **2** inspire **3** convinced **4** emphasize
B **1** theory **2** abstract **3** surgeries **4** fleeting **5** energetic **C** **1** b **2** a

unit 20 MEDICINE

pp. 84-87

★*New Medicine*

1 a **2** c **3** b **4** They break down at different speeds. **5** b **6** 1) F 2) F

아프거나 다치면, 의사를 찾아가는 것이 당신을 낫게 할 수 있다. 그러나 거의 모든 사람이 병원에서 좋아하지 않는 한 가지가 있는데, 바로 주사를 맞는 것이다.

그런데 현재 과학자들이 여러 다른 종류의 약품과 알약과 더불어, 마침내 주사를 대체할지도 모르는 무언가를 발명해냈다. 그것은 종이만큼 얇고 대략 작은 동전 크기만 한 특수 마이크로 칩이다. 의사들은 마이크로 칩 안에 있는 특수 주머니에 간단히 약을 넣는다. 그리고 나서 그들은 그 마이크로 칩을 당신의 몸 안에 넣는다. 일단 안에 들어가면, 마이크로 칩은 딱 당신이 필요한 만큼의 약을, 정확히 필요한 때에 방출한다.

어떻게 그것이 이렇게 할까? 각 주머니는 폴리머라고 불리는 각각 다른 종류의 물질로 밀봉되어 있다. 이 여러 폴리머들은 체내에서 다른 속도로 분해되기 시작한다. 그것들이 완전히 분해되면 약이 방출된다. 이것이 의사가 타이밍을 조절할 수 있게 해준다.

아픈 주사를 피할 수 있게 해주는 것 외에도, 이 새로운 기술에는 몇 가지 중요한 이점이 있다. 우선 첫째로, 환자가 언제 약을 먹어야 하는지 기억하는 것을 걱정할 필요가 없는데, 바로 칩이 그들을 대신해서 기억하기 때문이다. 또 발생 가능한 질병으로부터 자신을 보호하기 위해 여러 번 주사를 맞아야 하는 여행자들에게 유용하며, 그것은 그들이 반복적으로 병원에 가지 않아도 되게 한다.

마이크로 칩은 다섯 달까지 약을 계속 공급할 수 있다. 그 후에는 안전하게 몸속으로 녹아 없어진다. 팔에 뾰족한 주삿바늘을 꽂는 것보다 훨씬 더 나은 것 같은데, 그렇지 않은가?

어휘   get a shot 주사를 맞다   replace[ripléis] ⑧ 대체하다   pill[pil] ⑲ 알약   microchip[máikroutʃip] ⑲ 마이크로 칩   place[pleis] ⑧ 놓다   seal[siːl] ⑧ 밀봉하다   break down 분해되다   save[seiv] ⑧ 구하다; *…하지 않아도 되게 하다   melt away 녹아 사라지다   needle[níːdl] ⑲ 바늘 [문제] undergo[ʌndərgóu] ⑧ 겪다, 받다   operation[ɑ̀pəréiʃən] ⑲ 수술

구문 2행   But there is one thing [**that** almost no one likes at the doctor's office] ....
- that 이하는 one thing을 수식하는 목적격 관계대명사절

11행   **Once** it's inside, the microchip releases just *as much* medicine *as* you need, ...
- once: '일단 …하면'의 의미의 접속사
- as much ... as ~: ~만큼 많은 …

20행   ..., patients **don't have to worry** about remembering *when to take* their medicine ...!
- don't have to-v: …할 필요가 없다
- when to-v: '언제 …할지'의 의미로, remembering의 목적어 역할을 함

22행 It is also helpful for travelers [**who** need several shots ... a possible disease], ...
　　　　• who 이하는 travelers를 수식하는 주격 관계대명사절

STRATEGIC ORGANIZER　inside, implanted, painful, timely, repeated

EXPANDING KNOWLEDGE

1 a　**2** *1)* F　*2)* T

인간과 마찬가지로 개도 병이 낫기 위해 때로는 약이 필요하다. 개에게 알약을 주려면, 다음의 기술을 사용해라. 우선, 이빨이 보이도록 당신의 개의 입술을 누르고 개의 입을 벌려라. 이제 개의 혀 뒤쪽 중간에 알약을 놓아라. 알약이 너무 앞쪽이나 옆에 있으면, 당신의 개는 그것을 뱉어낼 것이다. 그런 다음 당신의 개가 알약을 삼키게 하기 위해 개의 목을 문질러라. 아니면 개의 먹이에 약을 숨길 수 있다. 무엇을 하든지 절대로 알약을 으깨지 마라. 약의 분말의 좋지 않은 맛이 개가 약을 삼키기 더 어렵게 하고, 그 방법이 덜 효과적이게 할 수 있다.

어휘　get over 회복하다, 극복하다　　forward[fɔ́ːrwərd] ⨦ 앞으로, 앞쪽에　　spit out 뱉다
　　　throat[θrout] ⨦ 목　　swallow[swálou] ⨦ 삼키다　　alternatively[ɔːltə́ːrnətivli] ⨦ 그 대신에, 그렇지
　　　않으면　　crush[krʌʃ] ⨦ 가루로 만들다　　strategy[strǽtədʒi] ⨦ 전략, 방법　　effective[iféktiv]
　　　⨦ 효과가 있는　　[문제] proper[prápər] ⨦ 적합한　　medicate[médəkèit] ⨦ 약을 투여하다

구문　8행　**Whatever** you do, never crush the pill.
　　　　　• whatever: '무엇을 …하더라도'라는 의미의 복합관계대명사(= no matter what)
　　　9행　... will make **it** harder *for your dog* [**to swallow** it] ....
　　　　　• it은 가목적어이고, to swallow 이하가 진목적어
　　　　　• for your dog: to부정사의 의미상 주어

VOCABULARY REVIEW

A　**1** melt away　**2** place　**3** illness　**4** swallow
B　**1** get over　**2** technique　**3** up to　**4** seal　**5** avoid　　**C**　**1** a　**2** b